Spaceships in Prehistory

Also by Peter Kolosimo

NOT OF THIS WORLD
TIMELESS EARTH

Spaceships
in
Prehistory

by PETER KOLOSIMO

Translated by Lovett F. Edwards

UNIVERSITY BOOKS, INC.
Secaucus, N. J.

LIBRARY OF CONGRESS CATALOGING IN PUBLICATION DATA

Kolosimo, Peter.
   Spaceships in prehistory.

   Translation of Astronavi sulla preistoria.
   1. Interplanetary voyages. 2. History, Ancient.
   3. Man, Prehistoric. I. Title.
   CB156.K6413   1976   001.9'42   76-15670
   ISBN 0-8216-0256-X

First American Edition, 1976

Copyright © 1971 by Sugarco Edizioni, Milan, Italy
Translation copyright © 1975 by Garnstone Press and Lovett F. Edwards

Queries regarding rights and permissions should be addressed to University Books, Inc., 120 Enterprise Ave., Secaucus, N. J. 07094.

Published by University Books, Inc.

Manufactured in the United States of America

Contents

Eagle of the stars, vineyard of the mists . . .
Mineral serpent, rose of stone.
Buried ship, wellspring of stone.
Charger of the moon, light of stone.
Equinoctial square, vapor of stone.
Ultimate geometry, book of stone.

From the *Canto Generale*
by Pablo Neruda

Spaceships in Prehistory

I

The Descent of the Gods

Mario Salomone is a very strange man. So strange that he has chosen a hobby that is far from restful, that of time-travelling. He goes out of his studio or his house and disappears. He reappears an hour or so later. If we consider the matter from another viewpoint, centuries and centuries ago, in the times of barbarism, Mario Salomone seeks what interests him and then moves on into the Roman epoch. Or into prehistory.

Where has he gone to now? The age of bronze?

Perhaps. A few shards discovered here and there would suggest to him this date, however indistinct, in the mysterious calendar of our past. But nothing betrays the period in which he is in. The landscape of the Alpine foothills is marked by harsh outlines, by scrub and maquis, by a silence broken only by crackling twigs and trodden leaves.

From this lowering backdrop, almost evocative of unknown dimensions, rises the awesome summit of the Musine, that sinister mountain, about thirteen kilometers (20 mi.) from the spot where Turin now is, upon which nothing of beauty grows, nothing thrives and everything is rejected by uniformly hostile nature.

Our friend looks around, searching for some landmark.

Then, suddenly, he sees a "flying saucer."

It is there, not hovering in mid-air, but scratched on a rock, manifest and tangible, which is more than can be said

Fig. 1

9

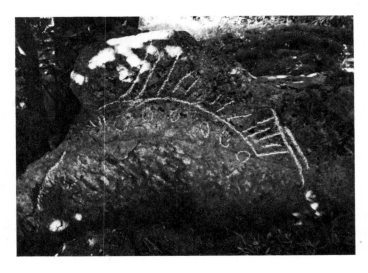

Fig. 1. The so-called 'solar rock' at S.Antonino di Susa in Piedmont. It could be compared with the Franco-Iberian rock carvings; the incised discs and the rays do not, however, correspond with any known solar image.

of the sights which continue to be reported from every part of the globe.

Science fiction in stone

Mario Salomone is a "time-traveller," as we have said, but nonetheless, is firmly anchored to our own times. In reality, his excursions through centuries and millennia are a task of passionate research carried on along the enigmatic paths of the past, traced out in the vicinity of Turin (in the Susa valley especially) by known and unknown civilizations.

Member of the "Ad Quintum" archaeological group,[1] Salomone tries, so much is evident, not to let himself be carried away by his imagination. He does not speak of a "flying saucer" but rather of a "Solar Rock," that is to say a solar symbol, but he cannot refrain from stressing a few particulars which would leave anyone perplexed.

"At about the five hundred meter contour, in a small wood on the western side of the 'crest' of Sant'Antonino di Susa," we read in his report, "on a rock 2.60 meters (8.5 ft.) long and sticking out of the earth for about 1.20 meters (3.9 ft.), can be seen markings in the form of an ellipse with lines about a centimeter (0.4 in.) in depth and two centimeters (0.9 in.) wide."

"It is an interesting fact that the line of the ellipse is overscored by other lines disposed in the form of a halo; at first they appear curved, then become straight and shorter. In the terminal section two clear incisions cross them, giving the idea of a tail.

"In the inner part of the ellipse, ten centimeters (4 in.) lower down, a series of smooth almost circular discs placed five centimeters (2 in.) apart follow the line of the curvature."

"The incisions face east, towards Mount Musine . . ."

"Face east" may, in fact, be interpreted to all intents and purposes as symbolizing the rising sun. We should not, however, forget that we do not know any other solar symbol with a pattern of rays of this nature, incomplete and lacking the frontal part of the ellipse, with oblique parallel lines turning to the right, so as to give an impression of movement. But where else in the world can be found a symmetrical arrangement of so many discs, recalling, without too much effort, a series of portholes. So many discs would have no sense in a solar representation!

Are we then faced with a prehistoric portrayal of a spaceship?

Perhaps one might smile at an idea of this sort, were it not that the markings at Sant'Antonino di Susa can be compared with others, sometimes less precise, but certainly sufficient to reveal a surprising similarity.

The researcher and explorer Aimé Michel speaks of this. He lists at least seventeen caves in what he calls the Franco-Cantabrian region which extends, more or less, from the zone crossed by the river Vézère (Limousin, France) to the Spanish province of Santander, where, among others, the famous mural paintings of Altamira are to be found. These paintings go back to an unknown culture which flourished from c. 30000 to 10000 B.C.[2] For the most part they are drawings of animals. Whoever it was who undertook the task of classifying them, listed, in seventy-two caves, 610 horses, 510 bison, 205 mammoths, 176 ibexes and more than five hundred other quadrupeds.

It is clear that the painters of this enigmatic culture (born artists, we should say, considering the naturalness, the perfection of line and the beauty of their works) attributed a very great importance to the chase. Something else, however, must have impressed them very deeply to make them insert other images among those mirroring the concepts upon which their existence was based.

These are images considered incomprehensible by scholars of prehistory; and so too we would have considered them until yesterday, that is, until men began to think about "flying saucers" and to reproduce their shapes.

Let us imagine that we are living on an isolated island. We know nothing of the rest of the world, but we are able to keep a diary. It is obvious that its pages would be largely concerned with descriptions of our own most immediate problems (which would be mainly concerned with food). If we should see a ship passing across the horizon we should devote a few, not many, words to it. But if the episode were repeated, if some ship should come directly to our shores and land upon them, we should certainly describe in an adequate manner an event which broke so brusquely and dramatically the tenor of our days.

Could not something similar have happened to the dwellers in those French and Spanish caves?

These palaeolithic artists, Michel remarks, "reproduced very faithfully whatever they wanted to depict. Their credibility is absolute." He continues, referring to the signs which they employed to represent various types of what

today we could call UFOs (Unidentified Flying Objects):
"If these works do not represent anything, then we must
ask ourselves how artists so bound to realism in every other
field could have expressed their fantasies, imagining in so
precise a manner and with surprising exactness those forms
whose existence was to be demonstrated fifteen to twenty
thousand years later by the 'Condon Report'."

The French savant offers us, cataloguing them, copies
of the designs made by Professor André Leroi-Gourhan,
the greatest living authority on western prehistoric art.

Fig. 2

Let us examine these reproductions. In our view some
of them are too uncertain for us to agree to include them
among representations of unidentified flying objects.
Others, however, are undoubtedly impressive, as is also
the fact that several designs identical or very similar have
been discovered in caves a considerable distance away.

Let us look, for example, at the designs in groups G, O
and P; we shall see, perfectly stylized, the most frequently
recurrent shapes of space vehicles of presumed extraterrestial origin, just as they are presented to us in the photographs and reconstructions of our own days.

In some of these drawings the idea of movement is expressed by a technique which we shall define as "comic
strip." Prehistoric comic strips? Let us cast a glance at
drawings O-11 and Q-11 and convince ourselves. G-11,
however, with that series of points at its base, seems as if
it were trying to convey the luminosity proper to the
UFOs!

"The G-6 type of signs (which appear again with the
letter P) are in the majority of cases on the roofs of the
caves, in every possible position, sometimes in groups of
two, three or four," writes Michel. "It is a significant fact
that the part of the roofs reserved for these objects is de-
voted exclusively to them, whereas the spaces adjacent are
thronged with animals, so crowded that sometimes they
are drawn one over another. One gets the impression that
the artists had agreed to stress the importance of these

13

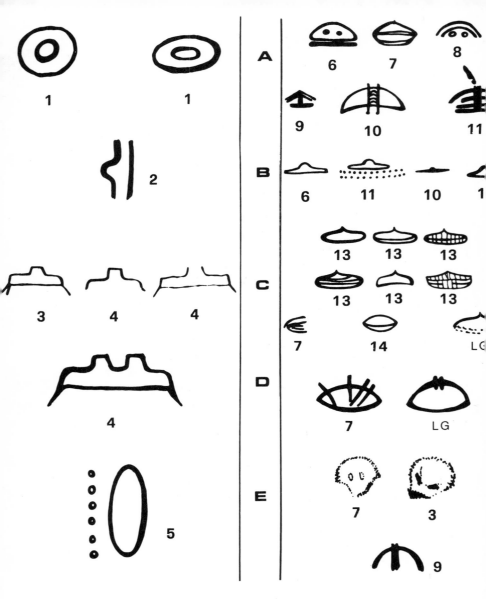

Fig. 2. These are symbols found in seventeen caves in the Franco-Iberian region by Aimé Michel, guided by the researches of Leroi-Gourhan. The letters refer to the classification made by Michel according to the vari-

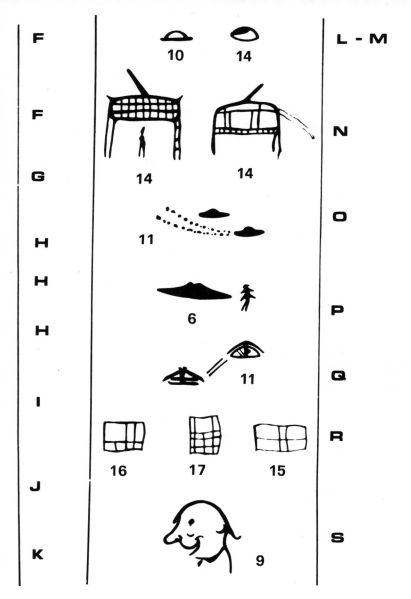

ous types of objects represented, the numerals to the places where the finds were made which are listed below. The approximate date of these designs is shown in brackets.

1. Pair-non-Pair, near Marchamps, Gironde, France (30000-20000 B.C.). Concentric forms (A-1)

2. Villars, Dordogne, France (c. 15000 B.C.). Symbol with lateral protuberances, perhaps comparable with those of letters C & D (B-2)

3. Pech Merle, near Cabrerets, Lot, France (c. 15000 B.C.). Symbol with upper protuberance, humanoid head (C-3, J-3)

4. Cougnac, near Payrignac, Lot, France (c. 15000 B.C.). Humanoid heads (repeated six times) and symbols with upper protuberances as at Pech Merle; in addition, a symbol with two symmetrical protuberances (C-4, D-4)

5. Las Chimeneas, near Puente Viesgo, Santander, Spain (c. 20000 B.C.). Elliptic form with six discs aligned vertically to the left (E-5)

6. Altamira, near Santillana, Santander, Spain (c. 12000-10000 B.C.). "Discs" recalling the shape of present-day UFOs, one of them with a figure alongside it (F-6, G-6, P-6)

7. Les Combarelles, near Les Eyzies, Dordogne, France (12000-10500 B.C.). Elliptic signs crossed by lines, some of which seem to resemble antennae; humanoid head which recalls J-3 (Pech Merle) (F-7, H-7, I-7, J-7)

8. Font de Gaume, near Les Eyzies, Dordogne, France (c. 12000 B.C.). "Roof-shaped" symbols (F-8)

9. Rouffignac, near Fleurac, Dordogne, France (12000-

10500 B.C.). *"Roof-shaped" symbols and humanoid faces which recall J-3 and J-7 (Pech Merle and Les Combarelles), human profile with some features which recall certain humorous designs (F-9, K-9, S-9)*

10. Les Trois Frères, *near Montesquieu, Avantès-Ariège, France (12000-10000 B.C.). "Roof-shaped" symbols, one of which seems to show a ladder. "UFO forms" (F-10, G-10, L-10)*

11. *Naux, Ariège, France (c. 12000 B.C.). "UFO forms," some of which suggest the idea of movement (F-11, G-11, O-11, Q-11)*

12. La Cullalvera, *near Ramales, Santander, Spain (12000-10500 B.C.). "UFO forms" (G-12)*

13. La Pasiega, *near Puente Viesgo, Santander, Spain (13000-10500 B.C.). "UFO forms" (H-13)*

14. Ussat, *Ariège, France (c. 10500 B.C.). Discoidal signs, a construction which reminds Aimé Michel of the American lunar module. The drawing is accompanied, lower center, by a human gure (H-14,M-14, N-14)*

15. El Castillo, *near Puente Viesgo, Santander, Spain (12000-10000 B.C.). Quadrilaterals with internal signs (R-15)*

16. Lascaux, *near Montignac, Dordogne, France (15000-12000 B.C.). Quadrilaterals with internal signs (R-16)*

17. La Gabillou, *near Sourzac, Dordogne, France (15000-12000 B.C.). Quadrilaterals with internal signs (R-17)*

unknown forms and to draw attention in every way to their nature, so different from anything in the surroundings in which the inhabitants of the caves lived."

Let us take another look at P-6. Alongside the disc we can see a very strange humanoid figure whose lateral appendages, like four arms, are clearly science fiction. Closer to our own genus is the little outline figure overshadowed by a most curious structure (N-14).

"It is baffling that men of the Magdalenian epoch, clothed in animal skins and armed with stone axes, could have been able to conceive objects so closely resembling machines resting on four feet and provided with antennae and ladders," the researcher comments, "and our astonishment increases when we look at the human figure, which gives us an idea of the dimensions of the overshadowing structure: they are the dimensions of the LEM, the American Lunar Module!"

Shall we go in search of these "extraterrestials"? Here is the first of them, in the immense labyrinth of Pech Merle (J-3). Aimé Michel describes it thus. "It has an enormous skull, a prognathous jaw; it lacks ears and its eyes are represented by oblique upward-slanting lines." Above this enigmatic figure is poised a strange object (C-3) in which the French savant believes that he can identify a flying machine; it is the same object that we see repeated six times in the cave at Cougnac (C-4), which is about forty kilometers (64 mi.) distant from Pech Merle as the crow flies.

Other strange gentlemen look down on us from the walls of the cave at Les Combarelles, accompanied by designs which are once again reminiscent of UFOs (F-7, H-7, I-7), the last of which, says Michel, appears to be provided with antennae.

Writing of these beings (J-7), Professor Leroi-Gourhan says, "Almost all the faces have an animalistic appearance, which leads one to formulate the theory that they depict men with beast masks."

Masks? Or are we faced with unknown races or even,

18

following the lead suggested by science fiction in its representations of flying objects, by beings wearing space-helmets?

But let us put a brake on our imagination, at the same time bearing in mind that human beings are depicted, in the graffiti and mural paintings of the same zone, in quite a different manner. As a matter of curiosity, let us recall the "Rouffignac manikin" (S-9) who seems to have been taken from a modern humorous sketch, but who has the respectable age of at least thirteen thousand years!

Cosmic coffins

A fiery streak furrows the night like a gigantic falling star and something swoops down upon the tundra in a hurricane of flame. The earth trembles and the vegetation around goes on burning until the morning. Then, when the pale sun rises in the sky, an unreal shape emerges from the curtain of fire still spreading over the area of the conflagration and moves towards the men who, panic-stricken, gather at a respectful distance.

The chief of the clan rises and, with incredible courage, draws nearer, brandishing a bear-spear and threatening the newcomer. Why a bear-spear? Because the unwelcome guest has a "strange pelt," a face like a wild animal with two large round staring eyes and a gait which recalls that of the plantigrades. The fearless warrior hurls his weapon, which strikes the other, but rebounds from its "fur," leaving it unharmed. In reply the "being comes from the darkness" lifts its paw (or its arm?) and its aggressor falls to earth, rigid, in the attitude he has assumed when he had rushed to the attack.

The shaman of the community, undoubtedly wiser than the impulsive war-leader, tries to appease the anger of the terrifying creature by offering it the most beautiful maiden of the clan.

Opinions differ about the reactions of "the monster which came out of the fire" (the legend, with many variants, is diffused through all northeastern Siberia). There is one version which says that it had no very strict moral prejudices and accepted the girl without more ado, and one which, on the other hand, describes it as an upholder of rigid principles and in no way disposed to yield to seductions of such a kind.

It is perhaps this version that has given rise to that curious superstition which regards the bear as a venerable personage, feared and hated at the same time. In whatever way the account is handed down to us, however, we note that it contains elements irreconcilable with the primitive cultural standards of the palaeosiberians. Trying to interpret it, we are tempted to see in the "strange pelt" some form of clothing (perhaps a spacesuit?), in the "face with the round eyes," which recalls the humanoid of the French cave at Les Combarelles, a mask or a helmet, in the clumsy gait the movement of a creature hampered by its dress, and in the paralyzing gesture the action of some weapon.

It is, however, a strange fact and even today the Siberian Yukagiri (in remote times they occupied an enormous territory between the rivers Lena and Kolyma, the Arctic Ocean and the mountain chain of Verkhoyansk, but are now restricted to a territory to the east of the lower course of the Indagirka, and are in danger of extinction) practise "hospitable prostitution," offering their women to their guests as a mark of friendship.

And it is among the Yukagiri that we may perhaps find the fantastic key to an enigma outlined thousands upon thousands of miles away in the Franco-Cantabrian caves.

When speaking of their pictures, we refer to them as "roof-form" graffiti. Sometimes these drawings have an oval upper section, but more often it is an obtuse angle. Let us go back to the tables of Aimé Michel and look at F-9 and Q-11; they certainly do not picture arrowheads, as some observers claim them to be, and this becomes much clearer in the second of these examples which seems to show an object in the act of leaving one of these "roof-shapes."

What can it be? Another flying object, or a scaffolding, or a type of hangar?

Let us examine the form of a "love letter" which the Yukagiri girls carved on birch bark, following a tradition handed down from time immemorial. The slender spear on the left certainly represents a man, the wider one to the right a woman. The outlines undoubtedly represent a house, the upper cross-beams grief and sorrow. The meaning can be expressed in these words: "You go away, I remain here. For you I weep and am sad." [3]

Fig. 3

But there are some who think that the meaning of these drawings may have been, in origin, something quite different, even though still an expression of sorrowful leave-taking: a leave-taking of the gods, moreover, who are abandoning their abode on earth to return once more to the skies from which they have descended. ,

For many peoples, in fact, a spear placed vertically means ascent towards the infinite. Even more; among many Tungus tribes (a people of Mongolian race which, occupying a vast area between the river Yenisei and the Pacific, has for some time past been assimilating the Yukagiri) we find what could be a direct link between the prehistoric drawings in France and the "message" conveyed in Fig. 3: an isosceles triangle with incomplete base in which an arrow is drawn point upwards. But this is not a question of a love letter but of a magic symbol indicating the mediation of the gods between heaven and earth. The "roof-form" symbol, in fact, represents the typical Tungus habitation, a conical tent or a semicircular yurt.

And the weapon pointing upwards? A spaceship, in the view of the supporters of the hypothesis according to which our planet was several times visited by representatives of advanced stellar civilizations in the remote past.

We already know that another Siberian people, living

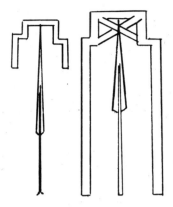

Fig. 3. The "Yukaghir love letter"; there are some who think it records a departure of visitors from space.

Fig. 4

in some of the valleys previously settled by the Tungus, the Yakuts, place the coffins of their dead on the branches of trees, to the chanting of a funeral dirge which says: "Sleep . . . sleep until the spirits descend from the stars in their shining chariots." [4]

Fig. 5

Let us add that this strange custom, with certain variations, is common to all the primitive peoples of this immense area of Asia: the Yukagiri place their coffins on piles, whereas the Tungus place them obliquely on scaffoldings which, however much one wishes to be a realist, suggests very strongly to the imagination the concept of "something" ready to spring up to the skies, to the dwelling place of the gods.

A missile?

It is a concept to which, whether we like it or not, we must pay heed, an idea perhaps expressed by works of various kinds whose primitive sense has become lost or deformed yet which preserve, often in obscure form, their original nucleus of meaning. This is the case with obelisks, campaniles and minarets.

There are some who, when referring to such constructions, would like to regard them as an unconscious imitation of ancient phallic symbols, but such an interpretation is absolutely unacceptable, as we believe we have already prooved when speaking of the Maya steles.[5]

To demolish this hypothesis it would be enough to glance for a moment at the obelisk of Tutmoses at Karnak, *Fig. 6* a monolith of red granite from the Aswan quarries in Egypt and about twenty-three meters in height.

What can we say, then, of another construction considerably nearer to us in time. We have shown the photo of it (reproduced here) to various friends and asked them pointblank what it represents.

"A missile," was the unhesitating reply. Nonetheless, it is a photo of the minaret of the New Mosque at Istanbul *Fig. 7* which gives the idea of a spaceship on its launching pad!

Fig. 4. The coffin of a Yukaghir child, erected on piles.

Fig. 5. Another strange burial place; this Tungus wooden coffin seems placed in such a way as to aid the ascent of the deceased to the skies.

The temples and the stars

Temples and spaceships: does there in fact exist some link between these two concepts apparently so discordant? Viacheslav Zaitsev, the well-known philologist of the White Russian Academy of Sciences who has many times thrown the scientific world into turmoil by his theories concerning the landing of "uranids" on our planet, states this decisively:

"My deductions," he writes in the Soviet periodical

Fig. 6. The famous obelisk of Tutmoses at Karnak; it is a monolith of red granite about twenty-three meters (80 ft.) high.

Neman, "are based on the idea expressed forty years ago by Nikolai Rinin, the friend and student of Konstantin Shiolkovsky who laid down the principles of the construction of space missiles and the undertaking of cosmic voyages at the beginning of our century."

Rinin stressed that there are stories in the mythologies

Fig. 7. A missile on its launching pad? No. The minaret of the New Mosque at Istanbul.

of various peoples which speak of the visit to Terra of intelligent beings from outer space. In 1959 this idea took form as a serious scientific hypothesis in the work of another Soviet savant, Modest Agrest:

"To the primitive inhabitants of our planet, these cosmic visitors must have appeared as gods provided with supernatural powers. If we presume that these gods came out of a machine (a spaceship), this would be enough to induce us to think that temples were constructed similar to it in form; and temples are common to all religions and all cults."

The so-called "apochryphal books" (Hebrew or early Christian books apparently inspired, but not recognized as such by the Church) tell us that David rose to the skies where the angels showed him the model of an edifice conceived as the future temple at Jerusalem. Returning to our globe, the famous King of Israel immediately ordered the building of this temple, which took place in the tenth century B.C.

Could the concept of the "church" have been, in reality, that of a spaceship seen by David?

Zaitsev asks this question and, recalling how the ancient Indian texts were much more explicit in their description of "celestial vessels" and of terrifying weapons, quotes what the Soviet writer Nikolai Brunov wrote about them in 1937 in his *Essays on the History of Architecture*.

"The symbolism of the temples of the great Asian peninsula has not been sufficiently studied. Their architects were the guardians of a forgotten saga, the deeper study of which would lead to a new, vast symbolic interpretation."

Obviously we do not know the structure of the alleged spacecruisers and, consequently, cannot establish parallels between them and the form of temples. Astronautics, however, seems to tell us that these extraterrestial vehicles must have been mainly composed of two parts, one of which was designed to overcome interstellar distances, the other to act as a tender between the spaceship in orbit and the celestial body chosen as its objective. We can see an example of this on a small scale by looking at the "mother ship" of the Apollo project and the LEM, the "lunar module" which breaks away from it to land on the satellite and then once more joins up with the mother spaceship.

Whereas the carriers could have been represented by steles, campaniles and minarets, it would not be absurd to see the tenders prefigured in the very many hemispherical buildings of antiquity, whose form has been identified by many scholars, as well as the Soviet ones, with that of "flying saucers." This profile, Zaitsev observes, in many cases recalls that of the *Vostok*, even as Phoenician architecture in many details recalls directly to mind the form of the United States *Gemini*.

We find the stele and cupola motifs united in the Indian *stupa* which is sacred to the holy places of Buddhism. "The most widely diffused form," Nicola Turchi says, "is that of a squared base made up of eight steps upon which rests a central body in the shape of an overturned pot from which rises a small tower subdivided into sections and ending in an apex with the symbols of the Sun, the Moon and fire." [6]

Buddhist symbolism lets us see, for example, in the large step-platforms, the steps which lead to illumination, in the "overturned pot," illumination itself, in the sections of the small tower, the representations of various religious concepts (the eightfold path, the ten knowledges and various mystical powers). It is, however, almost beyond doubt an adaptation to Buddhist elements which, previously, had a completely different significance. In the light of present-day scientific knowledge, might we not perhaps be tempted to see in the sections of the little tower the compartments of a stellar vehicle, in the "overturned pot" the space tender to which Zaitsev refers, in the symbols of the Sun and Moon the cosmic destination of a spaceship and in the symbol of fire its means of propulsion?

It is not, therefore, a simple flight of fantasy when

28

Fig. 8. A row of cupolas surmounted by pinnacles on the terrace of a temple at Borobudur (Java).

Zaitsev calls the terraces of certain Javanese temples on which are crowded constructions of this type "monuments to prehistoric astronautics." A similar definition could perhaps be applied, as Soviet savants also suggest, to many *tholos* [7] which appear to try to express in a horizontal sense the same concept as the *stupa*, joining the cupolas to elongated structures, "tenders" and "carriers."

The existence of similar buildings in various parts of the globe, very distant from ane another, is remarkable. It is enough to cast a glance at the temple of the Halaf culture

Fig. 8

Fig. 9

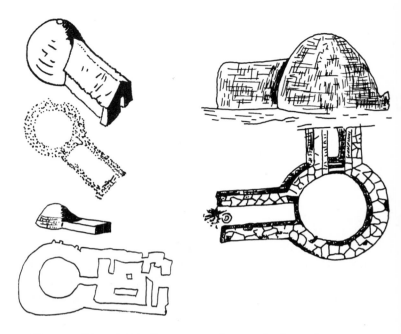

Fig. 9. (Top left) Reconstruction and plan of a temple in the tholos form of the Halaf culture (Arpachiya, northern Iraq). (Lower left) Reconstruction and plan of an ancient tholos temple at Mesara (Crete), built about 2000 B.C. (On the right) Sketch and plan of an Indian steam-bath. Note the remarkable similarity of all these cupola buildings.

in Iraq erected at Arpachiya and at a similar building at Mesara (Crete) dating back to 2000 B.C., or to one of the many Indian steam baths, in which the idea of purification is always linked to that of ascension and is often expressed by stellar symbols, recalling those on the *stupas.*

Fig. 10

If we examine the photograph of the famous "Caracol,"

Fig. 11

the observatory of the Maya city of Chichén Itzá, strangely similar to those of our own days, and compare it with that of the Dome of the Rock at Jerusalem, built by the Arabs in the seventh century A.D. on the spot where Solomon and then Herod the Great built their celebrated temples in all probability following earlier designs, we are astonished at the resemblance between the two works, separated by impressive distances in time and space.

The same may be said of the Mexican granaries intended for storing the maize harvest and built according to models whose origins are lost in the most distant epochs, of the villages of Harran (the Biblical city of Mesopotamia, "capital" of the enigmatic Sabaeans, where the cult of the Moon God was associated with the symbol of the crescent moon and the disc, later adopted by the Moslems), and of the tombs of the Marabouts from El Kasar in the Egyptian oasis of Dakla.   *Fig. 12*   *Fig. 13*   *Fig. 14*

From America to the Mediterranean: another great surprise awaits us within the framework of these remarkable juxtapositions. Let us look at the reconstruction of the temple at Tenochtitlan (the flourishing Aztec capital close to the present Mexico City) dedicated to Quetzalcoatl, son of the god of the heavens, Mixcoatl (Cloud Serpent), and the goddess of the earth, Chimalma (Shield Hand). It is an enormous stepped pyramid on whose upper terrace there proudly rises a huge conical construction surmounted by a strange ornament, which makes it even more similar to the *Gemini* than the buildings mentioned by Zaitsev.   *Fig. 15*

This building finds its exact analogy, though on a more modest scale, in the famous Puglian *trulli;* here we see the same cupola, very similar pinnacles and even the idea of the stepped pyramid expressed by the stairways which lead upward.

As for the emblems surmounting the *trulli,* we can see for ourselves how many of them could well be fantastic stylized astronautical symbols; the series of very curious spherical forms on the summits have led an American writer of Utopias to say: "I seem to see here translated into reality the panoramic fantasy of statues to space explorers which I have described in one of my books where   *Fig. 16*   *Fig. 17*   *Fig. 18*

Fig. 10. The "Caracol," the astronomical observatory of Chichén-Itzá (Yucatan). Its resemblance to the Dome of the Rock at Jerusalem is striking.

Fig. 11. The Dome of the Rock at Jerusalem was built by the Arabs in the seventh century on the spot where once rose the famous temples of Solomon and Herod the Great.

Fig. 12. These two Mexican domed containers for the maize harvest are constructed according to very ancient models and certainly reflect more permanent buildings.

the action takes place on a planet whose architectural structures are a monument to unknown cosmonauts." [8]

If this twinning between Puglia and Mexico appears incredible, we should not forget that striking analogies with the architectural expressions of distant civilizations have already been noted by many savants. This is what, *inter alia*, Enzo Minchilli writes: [9]

"The *trulli* . . . even though showing certain analogies with the Sardinian *pinnette*, the Istrian *casite*, the stone cabins of the Balearics and some constructions in the Dordogne, Navarre, Catalonia and the Ligurian Alps, Ireland, the Hebrides and Kurdistan, regions geographically similar because of the natural cleavages of their rocks, have in Puglia a peculiar character, displaying a typicl form, which I prefer to define as architectural purity, only in one particular area, having as it center Alberobello, the city of *trullo* constructed together with the communes of Locorotondo, Martina Franca, Cisternino, Castellana and Putignano.

"What origin must one attribute to this type of construction which pleases us so greatly and what is its analogy with those of other countries? Individual and differing responses have been given by those who have studied this problem and more than one of these seem to be the fruit of fantasy, but we consider it opportune to list them in order to throw light upon the references and the diversities of the advanced theories.

Fig. 13. The great area of domed dwellings of the mysterious Sabaeans (Harran). The analogy with the trulli *of Puglia is unmistakable.*

Fig. 14. Other buildings which make us think of the trulli; *maraboutic tombs at El Kasr, in the oasis of Dakla (Egypt).*

"Bertaux, for example, in holding that the *trulli* are anterior to the Roman civilization and even that of the first Greek colonization on the Ionian Sea, dates them back to the mysterious times of the Sardinian *nuraghi* and of the *talajots* of the Balearic islands. The *trullo*, Bertaux states precisely, is the most ancient type of construction that man has known, which in rocky districts, has taken place of the conical cabin made of mud and wattle. The cupolaed building, in the form of a flattened tower, is still today the primitive dwelling of some primitive peoples; the Eskimos build massive dwellings of ice-blocks, similar to the Puglia cabins . . .

"Chierici, however, goes back to Egyptian architecture, to the buildings of circular plan with defensive functions in the Mediterranean area and states that the influence of the rocky subsoil could not have had an absolute im-

Fig. 15. This must have been the fantastic temple built in honor of Quetzalcoatl at Tenochtitlan; note the cupola built on the platform of the great pyramid.

portance. It is rather the tenacious vitality of an elementary system through a period of thirty-five centuries . . .

"Drago asserts that the *trullo* repeats characteristic forms derived from primitive cultural cycles. The system of construction, however, is revealed as an innovation of advancing civilization and of a particular geographical ambient marked by an abundance of surface stone, and he records that there is evidence of the existence of the *trulli* from the time of the Normans. He does not, however, exclude the possibility that they may be the product of earlier civilizations . . .

"The extensive studies published on the Cameroons, Kurdistan, Spain and Syria, the ancestral land of the Hittites, make abundantly clear a close architectural analogy with the groups of *trulli* . . .

"The *trullo* construction, in my opinion, must have been imported by the Hittites in one of their Mediter-

Fig. 16. A significant view of the famous Puglia trulli.

Fig. 17. We are still in trulli *country; compare the upper part of the buildings with the upper part of the temple at Tenochtitlan (Fig. 15). Even the idea of the pyramid seems to be expressed by the steps!*

ranean migrations in the millennia before the birth of Christ into a very limited area, that of Alberobello, and it was developed successively as a building technique in the Murgia district, for technical and economic reasons."

What Giuseppe Cocchiara writes in the same book is also worthy of attention:

"Even today on the roof ridges of the *trulli*, symbols, signs and emblems which offer a rich field for the investigator glitter in the sunlight . . . Some of these symbols represent the signs of the zodiac and are associated with the astrology of the most ancient peoples; hence their magical-mystical or at least occult significance. For the most part, the symbols of this type are dominated by the circle which, in this specific case, represents the globe. It is true that at times the circle is surmounted by a cross which, even before becoming a Christian symbol, was used by many peoples as a prophylactic symbol."

Not merely prophylactic, let us add, recalling the development of the cross in Central America, where one sees it change into the lotus flower, into solar signs and into the swastika, just as in India.[10] And we note it on the *trulli* translated, together with the solar circles,

into symbols of known but enigmatic origin,

into the swastika,

39

into planetary emblems,

into the mysterious "Trident of the Andes," which recalls to us Poseidon and Atlantis,

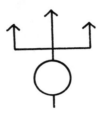

and into solar and stellar signs associated with the universal "tree of life."

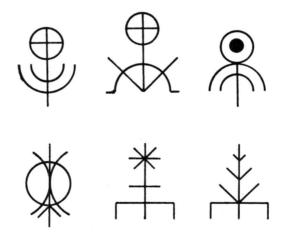

Fig. 18. The stylization of a spaceman? No. or at least not in the current conception of our own days; it is a line of trullo *cupolas surmounted by spheres.*

The ancient civilizations which flourished on all the continents undeniably have traits in common, traits which speak to us unequivocally of a single matrix, of very remote links, still living even if unknown to the bearers of those cultures, which were without doubt the heirs of other cultures still greater and more remote.

We believe that we have provided, in our earlier works, a certain number of elements apt to sustain these hypotheses which have led us to the formulation of fascinating theories; that relative to the existence of a highly developed people in times which for us are dateless, and those which search among the stars for the cradle of human progress.

We propose now to amplify these and to make them clearer, making use of the importance of photography.

II

Space-Thirst

The crowd stood in silence around the man with the lean emaciated face who, half wrapped in a strange dark pelt, stood upright in the center of the clearing.

"Friends," said the man, "I am about to leave you. I am going where my ancestors live, those who walk in the night and who fly from star to star. Powerful are my ancestors who plow the seas of darkness with wings of light . . ."

The man finished wrapping himself up in the strange dark pelt, lowered a mask over his face and slipped into a corridor leading to the entrance of a curious structure waiting behind him. As soon as he had disappeared flames shot out of one end of the structure.

What was this "dark pelt"? A space suit? Could the "mask" have been a space helmet and the curious structure a spaceship from whose jets darted a tempest of flame?

What we have been describing certainly lends itself to such an interpretation, supported by the words spoken by the mysterious visitor on his departure. But we are in a region of southern Mongolia, between the Altai mountains and the Gobi desert, and the protagonist of the episode was an aspirant shaman involved in an initiation ceremony. The "dark pelt" was that of an animal, the mask recalled the mythical Garuda bird [11] and the curious structure was a *yurt*, the dome-shaped felt tent of the nomads, which in this case was entered through a "corridor"; and the form of this Mongolian dwelling closely recalls the temple of the Halaf culture (northern Iraq) reproduced in Fig. 9, above and to the left.

And the fire? It was an ordinary barnfire to which was attributed a sense of purification, but certainly its most ancient sense, long lost, must have been linked to the words uttered by the aspirant shaman handed down to him across countless generations. Incidentally, we should not overlook the points of contact with the Siberian legend cited in the preceding chapter and the analogous traditions common to all the continents in which the "double skin," the masks, the shadows and the flames have a definite role.

Are we then witnessing a ceremony commemorating an astronautical exploit which took place many ages ago? The allusion is certainly suggestive; and we should not forget that we are in a region exceedingly rich in elements of what we may be tempted to call "science fiction" [12] and that very often, in every part of the globe, the religious or magical concept of navigation is closely associated with cosmic motifs.

Martians in Vietnam

Now we are on the rooftree,
We are high up, on the rooftree . . .
Blow, O wind from the sea!
Bear us over the Earth!
Blow, O wind from the coast,
Bear us over the Earth.
Row, O birds of shining plumage;
Use your oars, O vultures . . .
The rainbow is our means of transport . . .
The bridge-rails are of gold . . .

This passage (preserved by oral tradition and transcribed last century for the first time from the magic spells of a priestess of Toraja in Celebes) was recorded by Professor Anthony Christie of London University,[13] who translated it, relying on "the widely diffused belief in southeast Asia that the world beyond may be reached by descending the river or crossing the sea."

In a deeply interesting work of research, the professor has linked this "magic formula" with the bronze drums of the Dong-son culture (northern Vietnam), upon which

Fig. 19. One of the bronze drums of the ancient Dong-son civilization (northern Vietnam); as well as the spirals, the solar symbols and others difficult to interpret, there is a strange and enigmatic instrument in the center which recalls those of Valcamonia.

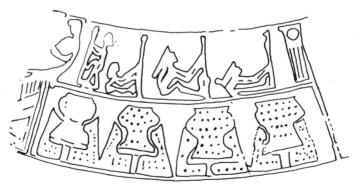

Fig. 20. Another drum of the Dong-son civilization; the receptacles below are totally unlike anything else in the culture of southeast Asia.

44

*Fig. 21. Dong-son once more. The strange beings with
feathers and folded wings suggest "spacial" images.*

can be found many scenes of embarkation. Are these means
for the transport of souls? Even if this should be, the concept could very easily be a transposition from a very
ancient plane of reality to a magical plane; but Professor
Christie himself provides another and even more fascinating interpretation: *"It seems almost certain,"* he writes,
*"that the boat is used by the spirit guide to communicate
with the kingdom of the living."*

A sort of ferry between Earth and the country beyond
the tomb? Or between Earth and space?

The hypothesis is undoubtedly daring. But if we observe the details of the designs and if we compare them
with others common to Asian, American, European and
African cultures of the past we shall find much to per-
plex us.

On one of the drums we see a profusion of figures,
perhaps plumed, certainly with bizarre head-coverings, the
tops of which are similar to oars and consonant to the
shape of the boat and to certain unidentifiable objects
which form part of some means of transport but which
have nothing to do with navigation.

Fig. 19

The Soviet scholar Leonov, referring to other analogous works in North Vietnam, suggests the idea of antennae raised skyward, basing his hypothesis on the many circles and the stylized double spirals, which are very probably solar emblems. It is worth noting that the beings shown on the drums have features which are only vaguely human and that the

Fig. 22. The enigmatic north Vietnamese "bell" with solar symbols and the "trident."

central personage is carrying an enigmatic instrument which which is completely similar to those held by the so-called "spacemen of the Valcamonica," [14] of whom another Russian researcher, Kazantsev, writes:

"Consider, for example, the rock carving discovered in an Alpine valley by the French archeologist Emmanuel Anati; there are anthropomorphic figures with strange 'headgear' which spring from their shoulders. They could by stylized images of the hermetic helmets of the 'foreigners'; also the external attachments of this 'headgear' are unusual. The figures grasp objects which . . . have the appearance of geometric symbols."

Fig. 20

Other representations have resisted all attempts at interpretation up to the present. In the upper part of one of these there are figures which some scholars interpret as four rowers and in the background four recipients. But here the oars end on the upper deck and containers of the type depicted here are totally dissimilar to those used at the same period in southeast Asia, as are also their most ingenious supports.

One might be led to think, rather, of beings grasping levers (nor is their attitude that which a team of rowers would assume) linked to storage tanks situated below them.

Equally indecipherable is the drawing of another four Fig. 21 personages who are working with unusual implements upturned over objects of a form never seen before. The hypothesis has been put forward that this represents two men intent on crushing something in two mortars, but nothing makes this acceptable; on the contrary we find here, though in a variant form, the motifs of feathers and antennae of Fig. 19. The clothing of the figures on the left contrasts markedly with that of the others; looking at the former we think of a symbolic motif of folded wings rather than a diadem of feathers and a short skirt.

The so-called "bell," recalling the bronze drums of Vietnam, is also devoid of any meaning for us. At its center Fig. 22 is another unidentifiable being, almost as if enclosed in a cabin with walls decorated with solar signs; beneath its feet there is something which is perhaps a trident, perhaps a "tree of life," perhaps a symbol of ascent, all of them motifs which place their seal upon the most fascinating enigmas of lost civilizations.

According to some savants the Dong-son culture could date back to about 150 B.C. Many things, however (as we shall see later when considering the enigmatic pictures of various prehistoric animals), make this dating very doubtful. Even if it were exact, we should in any case be driven to conclude that the Vietnamese of those times had preserved far more ancient records which have left their imprint.

Fig. 23. Longitudinal cross-section of the Etruscan tomb known as La Montagnola. It seems to represent with impressive realism a carrier and a "cosmic ferry."

We shall, in fact, find there the nucleus of the traditions expressed in Burma by the bronze drums with their plumed rowers, in Borneo (in Sumatra the dead live "beyond the ocean of the night"), as well as in Egypt, and the whole Mediterranean world.

The Mesopotamian crescent moon symbolizing a fabulous embarkation is a clear indication of space, but the Asian and American "batons," of which we shall find the synthesis in Tuscany, leave us truly astonished.

Fig. 23 Let us observe the longitudinal cross-section of the Etruscan tomb known as the Montagnola, which was discovered in 1959 at Quinto-Sesto Fiorentino. It is twenty-eight meters (92.4 ft.) long and was built probably in the seventh century B.C. The "carrier" and "space-tender" of Saitsev seem to be represented here with striking realism.

A "spaceship from the beyond," then? Yes, but a "beyond" which need not in any way be the abode of the dead. By adapting ourselves to "official science" and doing violence to our common sense, we could consider as a mere coincidence the fact that in very many Asian and Australasian regions (from Siberia to Indochina, from Polynesia to New Guinea and New Zealand), with languages and dialects differing completely from one another, there are the same expressions to designate "death" and "parting," "sea" and "sky," "infinity," "stars" and "another

48

Fig. 24. *The double spiral motif, photographed by the French film producer Lingé during an expedition to New Zealand.*

land" or "another shore"; but how are we to explain the similarity, phonetic, figurative and mythological, of the concept of "serpent" with those of "ship," "heavenly body," "obscurity," "life," "flight"?

In the most diverse manners, times and places, such concordance is lively and disconcerting, almost as if wishing us to say that the aspiration to an extraterrestial sojourn of the blessed "souls" was, from time immemorial, a yearning for flight, a lust for space, an ineradicable nostalgia, even if distorted through the millennia, for worlds upon which someone, in the unwritten history of humanity, has opened a spy-hole.

The era of the serpent

"Of all the decorative patterns of the Maori, one in particular struck me: the double spiral," (*that is to say* the spiral with a clockwise and counter-clockwise move-ment) writes film producer Gabriel Lingé, member of the French society of explorers and travellers, dedicated to

Fig. 24

49

Fig. 25

the study of the archaeology and folklore of distant peoples. "Repeated, with an obsessive frequency in carvings, paintings, woodwork, it also constituted in the past the dominant motif of facial tattooing.

"It is the same geometrical design found in photographs of a large number of galaxies. Today, the majority of savants attempting to solve the mystery of the origins of the Universe think that it was formed as the result of the explosion of a primitive, gigantic atomic nucleus,[15] whose fragments expanded throughout the cosmos in the form of a double spiral.

Fig. 26

"For many vanished civilizations (among them the Celtic) the double spiral, drawn, sculptured or engraved on stone was the symbol of the creation of the Universe. Today, if the Maori are questioned about this, some will show surprise that such a question should be asked, whereas others reply in an evasive manner, either because they do not have the 'key' to this enigma or because the last of the initiates (assuming that some of them still exist) refuse to reveal it.

"However that may be, is it not a disturbing thought that the representatives of cultures to which both the telescope and the camera were unknown could have repeated times without number the representation of the process of Creation as it has now been conceived only after the most recent discoveries?" [16]

Lingé is perfectly right. The motif which impressed him so strongly in New Zealand dominates the Celtic civilization from the heart of Europe as far as Ireland, appears once again, repeated hundreds of times, on the elaborate vestments of the Oroki (or Orrocci, Oroccioni) of the

Fig. 27

Manchurian taiga and also on the ritual chalices of Hazor, the Canaanite center of northern Palestine which was famous in the nineteenth century B.C., and is prominent on

Fig. 28

the Danish shields and ornaments of three thousand years ago.

"It was the era of the serpent," sing the natives of

50

Fig. 25. *The double spiral recurs once again in New Zea-*
land in the lines on the face of an old warrior; another
photo snapped by Lingé at Marae.

Fig. 26. Multiple spirals decorate a great stone placed before a Celtic tomb at New Grange in Ireland.

Fig. 27. Multiple spirals on a ritual cup of basalt in the Canaanite temple of Hazor.

Arnhem Land (Northern Australia), "the serpent which was before man, the serpent which was man, the serpent which flies in the skies." Two of these statements might seem a strange synthesis of the theory of evolution, the third remains Sybilline. But the whole refers to the Creation myth and the story of humanity, even though the aborigines preserve no record of this last.

It is just here that we find the origin of the symbol with which we are concerned; in the beginning was the

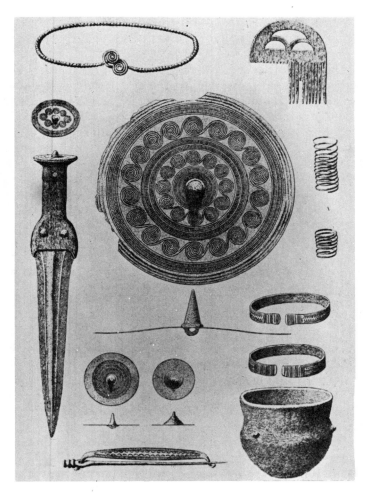

Fig. 28. The "eternal spiral" stands out prominently on Danish shields and ornaments of three thousand years ago.

egg (that cosmogonic egg which we meet with in the religions of so many peoples) from which was born the   *Fig. 29* serpent; the egg is the primitive atomic nucleus, the serpent rolled in a spiral undoubtedly represents the proto-galaxy!

This concordance with the most recent scientific conquests is recorded, as we have said, in the most distant civilizations, known and unknown: it cannot be a matter of mere coincidence!

Fig. 30

The serpent coiled like a figure 8 (our symbol of the infinite) of pre-Columbian America finds, for example, a strange concordance in the long interlaced coils of the Egyptian "serpopards"; and whether on this side or on that side of the ocean there is a hint of the spiral in the horns of the "sacred monsters" and the complete spiral is evident in the symbols of rule, diadems and badges.

Fig. 31

Fig. 32

We again find these scepters in spiral form which the so-called "astronaut of the Cauca Valley" (western Colombia) grips in his hands in the magnificent statuette recalling a man in a space suit, and once more in the golden pin of the late Bronze Age discovered at Tressen in the Saar.

Fig. 33

Fig. 34

Fig. 35

Fig. 36

It is these same spirals which, also in Colombia, mark the knees of another "prince" of the Cauca Valley, with equally enigmatic features. Similar spirals decorate the head of a well-identified cacique of Muisca (near Bogotá) and of his suit, and also frame the face of a mysterious Phoenician divinity of Ras Shamra (present-day Syria) dating back to the fifteen century B.C. and the breast of an Astarte, also Phoenician, of the fourteenth to thirteenth century B.C.

It is impossible to date the first rock spirals which can be found everywhere; we come across them on the North American mounds, in the Amazon jungles and in various regions of Colombia and Peru, seats of most ancient cultures, the main features of which we shall never be able to reconstruct.

These European examples dating from about twenty thousand years ago are ornamented, elaborated and inter-

Fig. 29. On the Vagnonville krater preserved in the archaeological museum at Florence one can admire this picture of satyrs intent on breaking the "cosmogonic egg" from which Gaia (the earth) was born.

Fig. 30. This little Egyptian tablet, dated 3200 B.C., celebrates, according to the accepted interpretation, the victory of Narmer, identified with Menes, the legendary first Pharoah. Note the "serpopards," the horned figures above and below, the stylized lotus and the spiral of the diadem.

55

Fig. 32. *The golden pin found at Trassen in the Saar calls to mind the Colombian spiral scepters.*

Fig. 31. *(Preceding page) The so-called "astronaut of the Cauca Valley" (western Colombia) gripping two spiral scepters.*

Fig. 33. Similar spirals (this time on the knees) in the portrayal of a "prince" of the Cauca Valley.

laced with solar symbols, such as those at Isturitz in south-   *Fig. 37*
western France. A similar juxtaposition is revealed later,
about 3800 B.C., in the ceramics which have come to light
at Nagada and at El-Ballas, north of Thebes (southern   *Fig. 38*
Egypt), which offer us a collection of ships, spirals and
disc-like forms which suggest overrash interpretations
which we could formulate only by linking them with
the graffiti and drawings of the Franco-Cantabrian region.
The same could be said of the Mycenean ceramics which   *Fig. 39*
go back to the fourteenth century B.C.

Wheels for land transport, anchors for seafarers, wings
for aviation. And for astronautics? As has already been
remarked (apart from the insignia—which differ—adopted
by the Soviet and the American astronauts) no "universal"
symbol has yet been found for the cavaliers of space.
Missiles have been assigned for the most part to military
units, the shapes of the Sputniks and Explorers are already
obsolete, and those of the present cosmic vehicles will
soon be outdated.

In America the spiral has been proposed, but rejected
because it has long been used, and abused, on the controls
of washing machines, dishwashers and other electrical
household gadgets. There were some who suggested linked
spirals, a somewhat ambitious design, given that we are
still pretty far from intergalactic voyages; a good presage,
however, which could also be interpreted as the meeting
of differing worlds.

We do not know if it will be adopted or not; we know,   *Fig. 40*
however, that it is not new. We first see it in the Sahara,
carved on the rocks in the times when that region was   *Fig. 41*
an immense and exuberant garden. It was, so we are told,
a magical symbol. For us it is undoubtedly so, since it
envisages once again fascinating questions; how could our
distant ancestors have known the structure of the greater
number of galaxies?

Granted that they knew it (since we have not succeeded
in explaining why the spiral has unquestionably been

59

Fig. 34. The Muisca cacique in the center of a group of golden figures discovered on the Bogota Plateau: spirals in plenty, on his breast and on his temples.

adopted in various parts of the globe to symbolize space, the Universe and, therefore, the Creation), whence and from whom did they take the idea? Was it from earlier civilizations which had reached at least our own level of knowledge but which had been wiped out forever, with all their achievements, from the face of the planet? Or directly from visitors rained down from space who brought with them this and other symbols in order to make clear to the terrestials the basic ideas of astronomy?

Fig. 42 From the Sahara let us go to New Grange in Celtic Ireland. There we shall find the two united spirals already

Fig. 35. Spirals recalling those of pre-Columbian America
decorate the head of this Phoenician divinity from Ras
Shamra.

Fig. 36. A Phoenician Astarte from the thirteenth or fourteenth century B.C. with spiral forms on her breast.

Fig. 37. These spirals, associated with solar symbols, date back to twenty thousand years ago. They were found at Isturitz in southwestern France.

Fig. 38. These vases with drawings of ships, spirals and even discoidal forms which suggest interpretations too audacious to be acceptable were discovered at Nagada and at El-Ballas (southern Egypt).

Fig. 39. Designs as evocative as the Egyptian ones have
been found on Mycenaean ceramics of about the fourteenth century B.C.

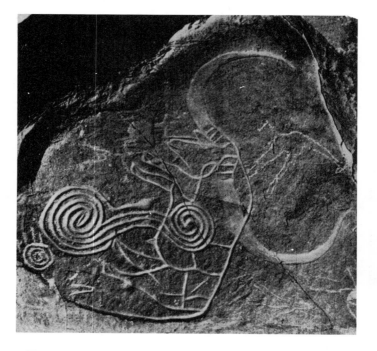

Fig. 40. A double spiral of the Tassili (Wadi Djerat).

Fig. 41. Another double spiral found in the Tassili.

Fig. 42. An Irish double spiral from New Grange (1) and one from Hal Tarxien in Malta (2).

1

2

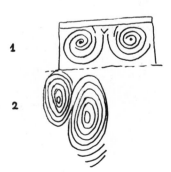

stylized so as almost to give us the idea of two enigmatic eyes. And the transition to this stylization is more than evident at Hal Tarxien, where the Maltese culture, which has been such a headache for the researchers of the past, at one time flourished. Here we see symbols in spiral form "like a serpent's mouth" alongside the "eyes."

Fig. 43

We shall find these "eyes" again in the *jomon* and *ainu* decorations in the equally mysterious prehistory of Japan, on Easter Island as a representation of Makemake, the god of Creation, associated with the Sun cult and in those disturbing personages with cat-like features, the so-called cat-men, who have left their imprint on all the civilizations of pre-Columbian America.[17]

Fig. 44

Let us visit New Guinea where we shall find a hint of the spiral to form the eyes of the masks made to cover the skulls of slaughtered enemies. These masks remind us, because of their cylindrical structure, of the upper part of certain space-helmets which have become familiar to us through science fiction illustrations.

In this way they express a feeling of respect for the dead adversary; perhaps similar to that respect which, in the legends, surrounds the "spirits of the night" which appear in the jungle and are slaughtered by the Papuans who, however, honor them, claiming to have wrestled from them "the secret of the Sun" (probably fire) and the art of hunting.

Spirals, Sun, hunting: in Valcamonica these motifs are united, though in a different and more suggestive manner. Engraved on the "Borno Rock" they seem to give human semblance to a rock carved by nature in the form of a skull (doubless a cult object for the ancient inhabitants of this area) and unite the concepts of a baffling culture with fabulous stellar allusions.

Fig. 45

Nor, to end with, is the link with America lacking. The "eyes of Makemake" seem reflected, scores of times, in the famous Mayan Copán vase (Honduras), converging

Fig. 46

g. 43. (Preceding page) Spirals, sometimes accompanied by serpentiform symbols, sometimes imitating em and sometimes in "spectacle" form, at Hal Tarxien (Malta). Official dating is from 2000-2400 B.C.

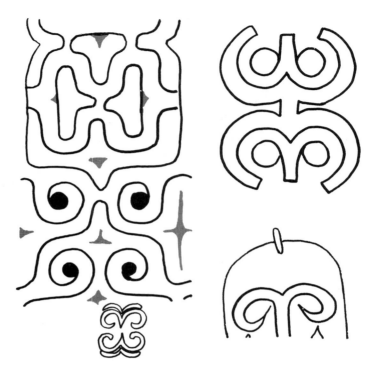

Fig. 44. (Left) "Spectacle" spiral forms, Japanese. (Upper right) Stylization of the Easter Island god Makemake. (Lower right) This mask from New Guinea, which might be called "spacial," is placed on the head of a slaughtered enemy.

on the center between handles with feline traits to form the features of an unknown god.

The fangs of the Sun

For those enamored of Utopian tales, the theme of the "return to Earth" is always among the most fascinating. It deals, in general terms, with a boy on board a spaceship who abandons more or less willingly his native planet (en

68

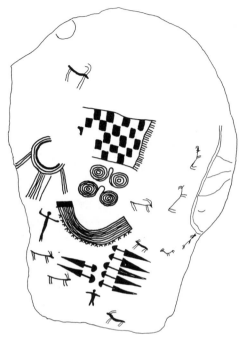

Fig. 45. The so-called "sacred stone" of Borno in Val-camonica; surrounded by a line which seems to suggest a skull. There are solar symbols, "spectacles" spirals and other symbols which occur throughout the world.

route to another) in order to return in what would be for us a distant future. He has travelled at a speed close to that of light, yet on his return many things have changed; and our survivor will change many more, handing down to his descendants the scientific treasures which he has come to know during his sojourn in a more highly advanced world.

Among the innumerable variations one of the most fascinating is that of the hero snatched away at an early age and then sent back as an adult to his own planet, which obviously seems to him a totally alien place. In their turn the terrestials regard him as a sort of god, bearer of the most precious knowledge.

We must, however, point out that science fiction was not born yesterday. We apologize to the modern pioneers but, without taking any of their merit from them, we must stress, within the framework of our study, that the rough outline of many space fables may be sought in the most ancient times.

Fig. 47 In Arnhem Land the legend of Creation, expressed by evocative pictures on bark, is based on the motif of a serpent which, after having swallowed a boy, rises into

Fig. 46. On the famous Copán (Honduras) vase, the spirals converge between the handles with feline features to form the face of an unkown god.

70

Fig. 47. (Opposite) The "serpent creator" from Yrk (Arnhem Land).

the skies, then once more descends and gives the Earth its origins, creating plants, animals and man.

In this fable there is an evident discordance; how could the boy exist before the human race was created? But it is only an apparent contradiction, born of a simplification of the myth. Let us listen to other tales from the same region and we shall learn that, in reality, something pre-existed, a chaotic mass in which the future human beings "were confounded with the animals and the plants." In practice, therefore, the serpent (which brought its "prey" back to Earth alive) limited itself to putting the world to rights, assisted in that task by the boy himself. One might say that the boy had been snatched away only in order to be educated to become the guide and master of humanity which, previously, had merely vegetated upon the face of the earth.

Among the Chinook redskins of the state of Washington, the mythical reptile bore into space Aqas-Xena-Xenas, "the boy who reached the Evening Star (Venus) and married the Moon" in order to return and put the affairs of our planet in order, where as among the Kiowa (Kansas, Oklahoma, Texas) it is a very beautiful virgin who is initiated into astronautics: the woman "rises into the night, marries a star and comes back to earth with her celestial son," destined to give to men the treasures of knowledge.

For the aborigines of northwestern Australia, on the other hand, there is no take off; the serpent comes from the skies bringing with it beings which these people consider as their ancestors. They represent them in shapes called *wandjina*, with mouthless faces and heads surrounded by a sort of halo which has led several avant-garde savants to like the concept thus expressed with that of individuals wearing space-helmets.

It was in ancient Mexico, however, that the serpent myth was presented with the most amazing cosmic allusions. We have already stressed this in previous works but it seems to us that it would be interesting here to com-

Fig. 48. A Toltec stele clearly representing a divinity (perhaps Quetzalcoatl) emerging from the mouth of an animal with a forked tongue.

pare this with the conclusions and evidence provided by Roberto Calcagno, a young researcher from Turin.

"Quetzalcoatl, the god who raised Mexico from ignorance and primitive squalor," he writes, "is pictured in almost all the sculptures at the moment of emerging from the jaws of a serpent. It is not an ordinary serpent, however, since its body is covered with long, colored feathers. The man, the bird, the serpent, all lose their respective individualities and merge to an extent that they may no longer be considered separate entities.

"At this point it is reasonable to ask what could have driven the human mind to place Quetzalcoatl in so strange a situation, to confer on a scaly, creeping reptile characteristics so antithetical as feathers, to unite the attributes to which we have referred in so enigmatic a communion.

"Perhaps the answer must be sought outside the commonplace and over-rigid classifications of official science. It is a disconcerting answer, but it is supported by too many factors to be entirely dismissed. It is probable that the mythical personage reached the Earth on board a spaceship.

"How could a primitive people or, at best, a people at a very low stage of development better represent a shining and tapering spaceship if not by associating a serpent with a bird? The first has the form, the second the gift of flight. And there is more to it; in the pre-Columbian language *Quetzal* meant a bird and *Coatl*, a serpent.

Fig. 48

"The 'disembarkation' has been carved in a masterly manner on a stone at Yaxchilán. The god emerges, as is usual, from the mouth of the reptile; his head is covered by a very strange 'helmet' provided with many unidentifiable 'instruments,' completely different from those of the priests and from any other headgear.

Fig. 49

"In other steles, found at Xochicalco, the theme remains unchanged but the form is altered. The face of Quetzalcoatl, compressed in an oval bounded by the forked tongue and by the teeth of an animal, has an enigmatic expression. The impression is realistic, as if one is being watched by someone gazing through a porthole. At Tula, Chichén-

74

Fig. 49. (Opposite) A head emerges from the mouth of a serpent; it is at Xochicalco, but the impression is similar to those of Tula and Chichén-Itzá.

Itzá, Uxmal, the same representation recurs everywhere, with similar features."

Let us take note, in these representations, of the tongues of fire and the ever present spirals of which we have just mentioned. What are we to say, then, of the flames pouring out of some of the bizarre attributes of Quetzalcoatl as he is pictured in the so-called Codex Fiorentino (Book III) before his disappearance?

Fig. 50

Fig. 51

Xiuhcoatl is another "flaming serpent," a double of and a derivative of Xiuhtecuhtli, the god of fire who "aids the Sun in its course across the skies." Having already made the acquaintance of Quetzalcoatl, it does not surprise us to see him pictured with talons and with symbols representing the heavenly bodies which give us life and, perhaps, the constellations, as we are not surprised by the fangs associated with indubitably human articulations carved by another unknown artist.

Fig. 52

In the arid zones of northern Mexico, Calcagno goes on to say, can be found very strange stylizations of the reptile, similar to those found in Amazonia and Liberia. The animal not only shows internal "compartments" but appendages which evoke ideas of landing undercarriages!

These are graffiti which date back to the archaic period of pre-Columbian America. The rigid serpent, however, is pictured in various manners in all parts of the world. We recognize it in prehistoric times, in the so-called "command batons" of northern Europe and in the mysterious artifacts of the Trentino, whose use is unknown to us.

Fig. 53

In some regions it is transformed into a magic springboard into space. Another that is particularly suggestive has been photographed by another Turin enthusiast, Professor Lamberto Camerini, in the Vicinity of Algajola in Corsica. Though eroded into bewildering forms by the weather, it rises from a rock overhanging a cavern doubtlessly carved out partly by nature and partly by the "improvements" of man.

Fig. 54

Fig. 55

This ageless monument is comparable with another in

76

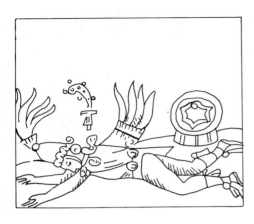

Fig. 50. Quetzalcoatl immediately before his departure, according to the Codex Fiorentino (Book III); note the flames, the "helmet" and the strange clothing.

Piedmont discovered by Mario Salomone in the vicinity of Caprie (Valle di Susa). It is called, in dialect, "the stone that looks" and it looks in truth into the void over a precipitous overhang.

Fig. 56

A work of chance, or an eccentricity of nature? Certainly not; if it were not sufficient merely to glance at it to be convinced, it would be enough to climb a little higher where solar symbols abound and speak to us of dark rites.

Fig. 57

A "sacrificial spur," therefore, from whose dizzy height victims were hurled into the abyss as a holocaust to the deified star? Or a kind of bold stellar springboard upon which the priest advanced, clasping his hands or raising his arms to the Infinite?

Perhaps both are acceptable; it does not need a great deal of imagination to discern the form of the springboard in the stone rostra of the grandiose Mexican buildings. Let us look, for example, at those of Chichén-Itzá, decorated with "enormous serpents" heads straining towards the stars. From the terrace of which it forms a part

Fig. 58

77

Fig. 51. Above and on opposite page: Xiuhcoatl is another "fire serpent"; here he is shown with claws, solar symbols and, perhaps, constellations.

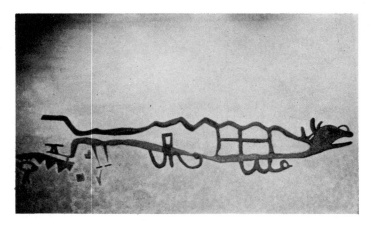

Fig. 52. *These very curious pictures of reptiles with in-*
ternal "sections" and appendages which directly remind
us of landing gear were found in the arid districts of
northern Mexico and are strangely similar to those found
in the Amazon region and Liberia.

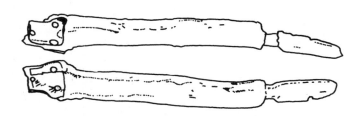

Fig. 53. *Prehistoric serpentiform artifacts from the Tren-*
tino; as for the so-called "command batons," their use is
unknown.

a jaguar's face fixes its gaze upon the Universe. It is the
"cat-man" of American myth, the creature "which came
from the stars." At dawn or sunset the fangs of the monstrous stone animal seem to close upon the Sun.

Fig. 54. The evocative "trampoline" photographed in the vicinity of Algajola in Corsica by Professor Camerini.

Fig. 55. The cave excavated beneath the "Algajola trampoline."

Fig. 56. It is very probable that "the stone that looks," discovered by Mario Salomone in the neighborhood of Caprie in the Valle di Susa, was at one time a "sacrificial trampoline."

We shall find the serpent as a symbol of immortality associated with Aesculapius, the Greek god of medicine struck by the thunderbolts of Zeus lest he take from man the fear of death, with Mercury (who as one of his duties accompanies the souls of men to the land beyond death), with the Caduceus, the famous winged staff.

Fig. 59 Here it is, once again in Mexico, with a head at each end, to represent an endless spiral. Another Pompeii in the Casa dei Vettii might almost be confused with the
Fig. 60 Aztec one. It has only one head, it is true, but in compensation it wriggles beneath the solar symbol, which brings us back to a similar significance.

Here it is in China, half-man, half-serpent, and in Meso-potamia, alongside the eternal and universal "tree of life,"
Fig. 61 the lions and the scorpions (symbols of existence beyond death), in the valley of the Indus, where a human figure

Fig. 57. Indubitable solar symbols were found close to the "Caprie trampoline" which show us that it cannot be regarded as a work of chance or a phallic symbol.

Fig. 58. The serpent and the stars: an evocative elaboration of the prehistoric "trampoline" in the Temple of the Warriors of Chichén-Itzá. Note the figure of the sacrificing ministrant with the feline head.

Fig. 62

Fig. 63

grips it in its hands (here too the feline element is not lacking) almost as if wishing to make itself master of its power and its force.

A similar lust for domination seems to underlie a metamorphosis in the unknown Danish divinity of three thousand years ago; the claws are transformed into serpents and the eyes assume an expression which, in truth, has very little of this earth about it.

Fig. 59. (Opposite page above) The famous Aztec plumed serpent, adorned with thousands of turquoises.

Fig. 60(Opposite page, below) The domestic altar of the Lares in the ,Casa dei Vettii at Pompeii. At the top the solar symbol, at the foot a reptile remarkably similar to the American plumed serpent.

84

85

Fig. 63. (Above) A Danish "serpent-god" of 3000 B.C.

Fig. 61. (Opposite page, above) The serpent, the scorpion, the lion and the "tree of life" on a kudurru, *a Mesopotamian boundary stone of the epoch of the Kassites.*

Fig. 62. (Opposite page, below) On a stone cup from the valley of the Indus, dated roughly 2500 B.C., a human figure holds two serpents in its hand, almost as if wishing to seize their power.

III

Sons of the Moon

The enormous bird circled slowly in the air. Its wings beat with a sinister roar, its smooth featherless body glittered in the sunlight. The huge monster was descending. Panic-stricken, the men, sheltering behind the trees, gazed at it from the edge of the clearing.

This must be a cursed spot. By night strange things appeared which moved in the skies, shining with a colorless light. The people avoided it, since the great hideous bird seemed to have chosen just this spot to make its nest.

The monster touched down, quivered and remained motionless. Silence fell over the clearing; even the birds ceased to sing. Then, without warning, some white figures appeared near the bird, as though they had come out of its body, and moved towards the forest. Some of the onlookers fell back. Others tried to do so but could not, paralyzed with fear.

Finally one of the figures broke away from the group and advanced, waving its hands. The men abandoned their hiding places and came towards it, shouting with relief and joy. They had recognized the being who greeted them; he was Momo Dakelhdivata Tasaday, the great Father-god of the Tasaday, who had returned to them riding a magic bird!

Fig. 64   This is not the reconstruction of an ancient legend, but

88

an incident which took place in June 1971, a discovery made by the Manila anthropologist Manuel Elizalde of a tribe which is still living in prehistoric times, in fact the Tasaday.

There are a little more than a hundred of them, settled near Lake Sebu, in the province of Cotabato on the island of Mindanao. About a hundred kilometers (160 mi.) away modern civilization is evident in all its aspects, but while their neighbors were watching the exploits of the space explorers on television the Tasaday were making the few tools which they use out of stone or bamboo and lighting their fires by rubbing two pieces of wood together. They knew nothing of farrming or stockbreeding, had not the slightest idea of metals, were unable to cure their sick and did not know how to count beyond twelve.

A casual meeting in 1966 with a member of another tribe who had entered their territory gave them a chance to learn how to make spears of bamboo and simple snares. Before that they had hunted or fished whatever they could with their bare hands. For the most part they ate palm pulp.

It was not strange, therefore, that they should regard the first white man whom they met as their one god (Divata the "father of ancestors"), the helicopter as a monstrous bird, and the phases of the moon as "the strange things which move in the sky."

The very dense forest was their universe, the sea a word without meaning (they had never seen it), the sky "a high thing" which existed "where there are no trees." During the first limited interview, carried on with the aid of members of a tribe whose language had a few elements in common with that of the Tasaday, a young man said, in substance: "We see the moon only when we are in some clearing by night, but we do not know what it is and it frightens us. The sun, however, we see more often but we do not know who owns it."

The man who could not exist

The discovery of the Tasaday, of this absolutely primitive people which until yesterday lived only a few steps away from the twentieth century without knowing it or being known by it (not, incidentally, the only example by merely the last in order of time) must warn us to move very cautiously in recording the history of the human race, its evolution and its progress.

Fig. 65

There are those who consider the Proconsul, which existed about twenty million yers ago and the Gigantopithecus (which lived from five to ten million years ago) as having "emerged from the same genetic origins and from whom later came men and the anthropomorphic apes"; and this could well be true. But the Plesianthropos of the Transvaal, which lived between two million and six hundred thousand years ago, which walked upright and had teeth similar to those of man, has nothing in common with us. The Australopithecus (about six hundred thousand years ago) and the Pithecanthropos of three hundred thousand years back are also alien to us.

Fig. 66

Fig. 67

By great good luck the theory, insisted upon by many scholars, that the so-called Neanderthal man was related to us and was among our ancestors has long been discarded. Even so, as we "anticipated" in *Timeless Earth* (1964), it has long been regarded as doubtful even by the most traditionally minded scientists and there have been many investigations to try and track down the survivors, if there are any, of the beings who from about two hundred and forty thousand to about one hundred and forty thousand years ago must have dominated vast regions of the globe.

In that book we printed two photographs of Neanderthal men who were discovered a few years ago in northern Africa by Professor Marcel Homet, the well-known Franco-German archaeologist and anthropologist. Of one, nothing more is known; the other, accepted by a com-

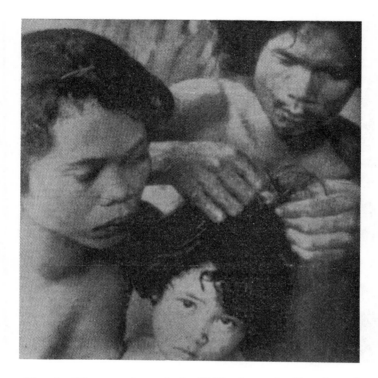

Fig. 64. *These natives of the Philippines, the Tasaday of Mindanao (whose existence was only discovered in 1971), live as in the Stone Age.*

munity settled in the south of Morocco and baptized "Azzo," has been dead for some time but has left descendants which were tracked down in August 1970 by an expedition of the CAI-UGET of Turin led by Emilio Henry, .the entomologist Alessandro Rossetto and the explorer Willy Fassio, with the invaluable co-operation of Dr. Alfredo Guillot, son of the Italian ambassador at Rabat, who too is an enthusiastic student of these problems.

"On the basis of the information courteously provided by Professor Marcel Homet to Dr. Peter Kolosimo," we

Fig. 65. A Plesian-thropos (above) and a Proconsul, according to the reconstructions in the British Museum.

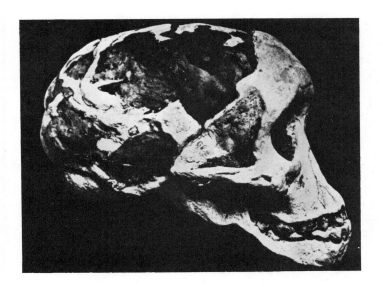

Fig. 66. Australopithecus Africanus, who lived about six hundred thousand years ago.

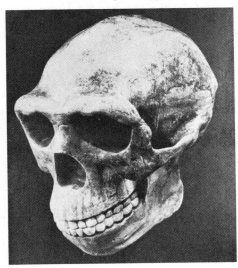

Fig. 67. The skull of a "Peking man" in the cast preserved in the Musée de l'Homme at Paris; he lived three hundred thousand years ago, learning how to use fire and to make rudimentary stone tools.

Fig. 68. Fig. 69. Fig. 70. Fig. 71. This photograph and the three which follow were taken by the Turin explorer Willy Fassio in the Moroccan oasis of Skura. They are pictures of the descendants of the last Neanderthal men, who are mentioned in Timeless Earth.

read in the report drawn up by Fassio, "we begin the most problematical part of our mission: the search for individuals with Neanderthal characteristics.

"The expedition thus moved southward to the edge of the Sahara, more exactly to the region of the oasis of Skura, near the Nei Dadés river, in a temperature which in a few days was to reach 55°C (131°F.) in the shade.

There we successfully pinpointed a small Berber village
named Iflan where we succeeded in approaching and
photographing (despite the Islamic prohibition) several individuals with very strange anthropological characteristics.
Insofar as it was possible, we tried to compile a short
history of the origin of this ethnic group, relying upon
information given us by the local inhabitants. This material was sent to Professor Homet to be worked up into
a more complete study."

As one can see from the photographs, some of which
are reproduced here, "Azzo's" descendants have been able,
even if only partially, to adapt themselves to the customs

Fig. 68
Fig. 69
Fig. 70
Fig. 71

of the community which has given them hospitality. Their
physical traits, however, remain such that, despite the
cross-breeding (possible in some cases, though not always,
by laws which require profound research), it is not possible to classify them in the ethnic groupings that we already know.

As we shall soon see, the surprises are only just beginning. Let us take a step or two backward; we shall find in
the Canyon di Santa Maria (Monte Bronco, U.S.A.)
traces of cavedwellers who already knew stockbreeding
and agriculture and who, after mummifying them (prob-

ably taking advantage of natural agents), buried their
dead in jute shrouds.

Traces equally ancient, if not more so, have been discovered in what has come to be called "the newest of the
continents." "Some archaeologists," writes the researcher
R. May, "date the Australian peoples back to more than
eight or nine thousand years. In their view Australia was
already inhabited by the end of the Tertiary, about a
million years ago. Human bones discovered in the Welling-
ton caves, in typical Tertiary terrain, seem to support this
theory. If this were the case, man would have appeared

Fig. 72. Among these rock drawings of the Valcamonica are some representing footwear.

there considerably before the appearance of the Java Pithecanthropos and the Sinanthropos of Peking.

"Today the Australian aborigines live as if they were in the Stone Age . . . they possess nothing and do not build huts . . . they have neither boats nor household goods . . . they know nothing of writing and transmit from generation to generation, together with their legends, the messages of a long distant past. On the continent there exist also graffiti and rock paintings." [18]

There are very strange graffiti: very strange pictures whose links with the artistic expression (if one may use such a term) of the present-day aborigines appear absurd.

"Absurd" also seems certain of imprints of footwear which date back to times in which man, according to official science, could certainly not have known any method of protecting his lower extremities from stones and rock. Among the rock carvings of the Valcamonica, we can see the very well-defined outlines of sandals, and

Fig. 72

Fig. 73. The so-called "Devil's footprint" found by Mario Salomone near Caprie (Valle di Susa).

Fig. 74. This imprint of a shoe sole was found in a calcareous stratum in Nevada. It undoubtedly dates back to a time previous to that established by traditional science for the appearance of man upon earth.

Fig. 73 the vestiges of something which very closely resembles shoes are impressed in the vicinity of Caprie in the Val di Susa (Piedmont); it was Mario Salomone who first drew attention to them. They are still called by the local inhabitants "the footprints of the devil." According to popular superstition, indeed, only the Evil One could have left his footprints on the rock.

Even more surprising traces await us in Asia and America. "In 1959," according to a Moscow review,[19] "on a sandstone rock in the Gobi desert the imprint of a shoe was discovered millions of years old which dates back to a period in which man did not exist. The members of the sino-Soviet palaeontological expedition, led by Dr. Chow Ming-Chen, who made this discovery were unable to provide any explanation."

Reporting this item of news, a savant added: "An imprint discovered in the Fisher Canyon (Pershing County, Nevada) on a calcareous rock of the Triassic shows the sole of a shoe with traces of stitching. Since it seems that footwear did not exist in the times of the dinosaurs, we must ask ourselves who was able to make such a shoe. Only two deductions are possible: either man appeared on the Earth millions of years before the date assigned to him by science, or that visitors from the cosmos had landed on our planet. These are two equally fantastic deductions." [20] *Fig. 74*

As are, moreover, those suggested by other findings quoted by Tomas:

"In the sixteenth century the Spaniards found a 7-inch iron nail solidly encrusted into rock in a Peruvian mine. It can safely be assumed that it was tens of thousands of years old. In a country where iron was unknown until recent times, this was truly a surprising discovery, and it is no wonder that the curious nail was proudly displayed in the study of Francisco de Toledo, the viceroy of Peru."

And again: "Ornaments of platinum have been discovered on the coast of Ecuador. This little fact raised a big question; how could American Indians produce a temperature of about 1770 degrees centigrade (3168° F.) thousands of years ago? Europe achieved this but two centuries ago." [21]

No one, moreover, has been able to throw any light on the composition of a bell-shaped vessel with floral designs inlaid with silver, of absolutely indeterminable age, which was discovered by chance as the result of an explosion near Dorchester in Massachusetts; it was of a totally unknown metal.[22]

We have already alluded, in *Timeless Earth*, to the skull of a prehistoric aurochs pierced by a hole which appears to have been made by a projectile. Professor K. Flerov, director of the Palaeontological Museum of the Soviet Academy of Arts and Sciences, speaks of it thus: "There

Fig. 75. The skeleton of a mammoth-hunter of thirty-five thousand years ago found at Vladimir in the Soviet Union; he was tall and agile and wore trousers and hide shoes.

are still Soviet researchers today who rack their brains over finds which merely add to those which years ago aroused questions which have never been answered."

"Bones of prehistoric ostriches, camels and hyaenas," states the review already quoted,[23] "were discovered in 1960 in the caves at Odessa by T. S. Gritsai and I. J.

Yatsko. They are about a million years old, but what concentrated the interest of scholars was that they had been cut into pieces in an exceptionally skillful manner. The borings are perfectly circular, the grooving regular. According to the experts, the bones must have been cut by metal instruments and later polished. But, according to accepted opinion, individuals capable of carrying out such operations did not exist a million years ago! Who, then, cut these bones?"

The discussion was resumed after the examination of the skulls of some mammals; and it must be extended into America by linking it with comparatively recent finds. The "Folsom projectiles," for example (so called from the remains near which they were found, which were those of the "Folsom man" who lived in New Mexico eleven or twelve thousand years before Christ), left a deep wound in the form of a neat slot. They are of stone, only five centimeters (2 in.) long, similar to a lance-shaped leaf; they were not arrowheads or javelin tips, yet they were used for hunting big game and had an exceptional force of penetration. How were they launched?

There is, for the moment, no answer even, as no explanation exists for the "Clovis projectiles" found from 1932 onwards along the border between Texas and New Mexico, and then also to the west of Naco in Arizona. These are from ten to twelve centimeters (4.8 in.) long and date back ten to thirteen thousand years (but those of Louisville in Texas seem to be at least thirty-seven thousand years old!). How did they manage to penetrate the skull bones of a mammoth? No one, so far, is able to explain.

The Maya and the elephants

Let us look at the hunter of mammoths; a complete skeleton was found intact at Vladimir in the Soviet Union. *Fig. 75* He lived thirty-five thousand years ago, was tall, active and goodlooking, wore trousers and hide shoes. His image is very, very different from that which some scholars have left us of primitive man. It may well happen that we shall find him again, in even more remote times when, so traditional science informs us, man "should not" have

Fig. 76. Designs from the Vietnam Dong-son culture seem to represent, in great part, animals believed extinct before the appearance of man.

existed, when no one could have known animals extinct before the arrival of intelligent beings on Earth.

Fig. 76   Nonetheless, if we return to the Vietnamese bronze drums we cannot do less than express some doubts about this. On them we see, for example, a member of the deer family which, with its spreading antlers, does not fit into the time or place when and where it "should be," and two reptiles (or amphibians) which, rather than crocodiles, recall the vertebrates of a very distant prehistory. The animal in the first row, in fact, resembles the reconstruction of the *Kotlassia*, typical of the Permian (more than two hundred and twenty-five million years ago), whereas that in the second row, with its elongated muzzle and caudal fins, is near enough in form to the *Archeria*, which lived

Fig. 77. A strange creature similar to a saurian; from the Como museum.

in the Carboniferous age more than two hundred and eighty millions years ago.

The "fish" seems in reality an ichthyosaurus of the Triassic (more than one hundred and ninety-five million years ago), the *Omphalosaurus;* the winged creature on the upper left reminds one of the famous *Archaeopteryx* of the late Jurassic (about one hundred and thirty-seven million years ago), that on the upper right of the ferocious *Phororhachos*, a carnivorous bird which lived in southern America (perhaps until three million years ago), about three meters (10 ft.) in height, and below that the *Ichthyornis* of the Cretacean (more than sixty-six million years ago).

These datings are impressive and it is very difficult to accept the idea that there should have been transmitted to epochs relatively close to our own the shapes and forms of animals which lived when the appearance of the first hominids upon Earth was not even a distant presage.

Fig. 78. On the "Stele B" at Copán in Honduras two elephants are pictured, back to back, with mahouts riding them. The outline was drawn by the British scholar Alfred P. Maudslay.

Fig. 79. The only complete skeleton of a cave-bear; it was found in Switzerland at 1447 meters (4,775 ft.) above sea level and is on show in the Saint Gallen museum.

We may very well have to deal with distortion by unknown artists which suggests to us quite unintentionally the juxtapositions to which we have referred. But if it is not a question of distortion, at least partially, what can we say about somewhat similar figures found in other Asian regions, in Africa and in Southern America?

If so, after taking into account that the datings quoted are nonetheless very imprecise, only two hypotheses remain open.

The first is based on the proved survival, beyond the periods laid down by traditional palaeontology, of some prehistoric creatures. Let us recall, in this connection, the uproar aroused by the capture of the Coelacanth which was believed to have been extinct for five hundred million years, of the *Vampyroteuthis infernalis*, and of the "Panama mollusc," regarded as having disappeared one hundred and seventy and three hundred million years ago respectively.

The second hypothesis is even more sensational and involves the existence of intelligent and highly developed beings in very remote times. Official science persistently denies this, but we cannot close our eyes to the roof-tiles and paved floors found in the same geological strata as the American three-toed horse which existed from about thirty to six million years ago, to the imprint of a human foot at Cow Canyon in Nevada dating back to thirty million years ago or to the most spectacular representations of animals which lived between one hundred and eighty-five to one hundred and thirty million years ago discovered by Daniel Ruzo at Marcahuasi.

To these facts, already set out with all the particulars in earlier works, we can now add others which we regard as equally interesting.

In the ornamentation which decorates the "stone calendar" of Tiahuanaco, the Frenchman, Denis Saurat, famous for his theories on gigantism, claims to have recognized the heads of toxodons, animals considered to have disappeared in South America at least three or four million years ago; and it is significant that there have been found just the remains of that great herbivore in a higher stratum than human bones.[24]

Tomas, for his part, has stirred up a discussion about a find to which official science has insisted on closing its eyes since 1924, the year in which the Doheny archaeological expedition uncovered in the Hava Supai Canyon (north Arizona) a rock painting of unknown origin resembling a tyrannosaurus. These mummifiers of knowledge believe that they have been able to cut the Gordian knot by affirming that this carnivore, the largest existent on Earth, became extinct about sixty million years ago. But it is a little difficult to decapitate a tyrannosaurus pictured in unequivocal form! [25]

Another design, at Big Sandy River in Oregon, brings us face to face with a Stegosaurus, which lived even earlier, about a hundred and thirty million years ago. And what are we to say of the pterodctyl which greets us over an abyss of millions of years from the ornamentation of a Cocle spiral vessel found in the vicinity of Panama?

All quite impossible, naturally. How absurd it is to think that an artist of the Dark Ages would be able to reproduce prehistoric monsters whose appearance is known to us only from the long researches and meticulous studies of modern experts!

Nonetheless, by a very strange coincidence, these monsters look down on us from the great cathedrals, from ancient castles and from museums. The Soviet savant Agrest claims to have been able to identify in these representations hundreds of animals which existed in reality millions and millions of years ago. We stand amazed before a stone creature like the one in the Como museum and ask if this represents a tyrannosaurus found in China in the deposits of the early Triassic, the period which lasted from two hundred and twenty-five to one hundred and ninety-five million years ago.

Fig. 77

Many ideas will also have to be revised concerning the existence and distribution of the mammals of the past. The elephant, for example, "could not" exist, according to official science, alongside the monsters of the Secondary Era, nor "should it" be found in America in the last seven thousand years.

Nonetheless, as Verrill [26] reports from Panama, there were found among the traces of the Cocle civilization which bequeathed to us the picture of the pterodactyl a picture of an elephant with a long trunk, ears like great fringed leaves and a saddle on its back.

Fig. 78

On the so-called "Stele B" in Copán, Honduras, we see two pachyderms, linked back to back and mounted by mahouts. They are elephants; no one looking at them could have a moment's doubt. The high priests of knowledge, relying on the dogma, according to which the great proboscidae should have been extinct for millennia in the "new world," plunge into the ridiculous, claiming that they represent two stylized parrots!

Parrots with trunks, with curved tusks and ridden by three Maya warriors? It was not without reason that the learned James Leslie Mitchell voiced a suspicion that some traditionalist archaeologists had mutilated the right-hand figure to suppress proofs which contradicted their theories but without managing to complete their work of vandalism.[27]

But there is more: at Marcahuasi, the enigmatic desert

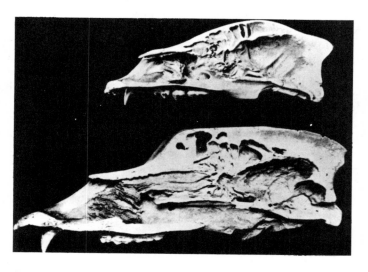

Fig. 80. (Above) The skull of a brown bear of our own times. (Below) The skull of a cave-bear which lived seventy thousand years ago.

plateau in Peru at an altitude of 3,800 meters (12,540 ft.), to the west of the Cordilleras, Daniel Ruzo found, alongside carvings of species extinct from one hundred and eighty-five to one hundred and thirty million years,[28] drawings of elephants, cows and horses, animals which did not exist in America at the time of Columbus's landing!

Divine bears

Mount Shasta, which rises to a height of 4,320 meters (14,256 ft.) in the Sierra Nevada in northern California, is a strange mountain. Not yet completely explored because of its hostile nature, it is the scene of mysterious phenomena which have given rise to fantastic rumors. Sudden gleams flash out on its slopes and fixed lights have become the source of innumerable legends; there is talk of "flying saucers," of a secret city inhabited by the heirs of an ancient civilization, if not actually by extraterrestrials. There are several travellers who claim that they have met in its snowdrifts curious individuals clothed in white, beings "not in the least human," creatures similar to yeti, gigantic, almost invulnerable bears.

"It was about three meters (9.9 ft.) long," recounts a hunter, James Barton, from Oakland, referring to just such a plantigrade. "To tell the truth, it did not threaten me, it even tried to slip away into the dense woods. Faced with a possible quarry of this sort, however, I could not but fire. I am sure that I hit the animal, but it only showed signs of anger. It rose on its hind legs, bared its teeth and stretched outs its claws towards me as if it wanted to warn me not to try again. Then it turned and unhurriedly disappeared among the trees."

Mr. Barton is also an enthusiastic palaeontologist and swears that he was face to face with an *Ursus spelaeus*, Fig. 79 that ancient inhabitant of so many caves. Nor is he alone in this: several other hunters with some scientific ideas on the matter express the same conviction when speaking of their adventures on the mountain ranges that extend from the northwestern United States into Canada.

It is true that in Alaska and on various islands which lie near it there are gigatnic brown bears (such as the Kodiak or *Spelaeus gygas*, the *Ursus arctos middlendorffi*) which can attain a length of from 2.80 to 3 meters (9.2 to 9.9 ft.), and weigh up to seven or eight hundred kilograms (1540 to 1760 lbs.), and it is also true that some of these plantigrades have migrated southward along the coast, but it does not follow that they reached the California mountains. On the other hand, the tales of Barton and his colleagues seem to be confirmed by gigantic fresh spoor found near Mt. Shasta, in the vicinity of Grant's Pass (Oregon), of Yreka, Redding and Red Bluff. Let us recall, moreover, that it was not far from this last center that the famous American "snowman" was filmed.[29]

Science places the period of existence of these cave bears between ninety and forty thousands years ago, basing its statements on finds which are very numerous in Europe. In the Swiss caves of Wildkirchli, Wildenmannlisloch and Drachenloch the remains of more than a thousand of these animals have been found; five thousand have been found within two hundred meters (660 ft.) of a cave known as the Drachenhöhle near Mixnitz in Styria in the Drachenlöhle itself a good fifty thousand, piled up in the course of who knows how many millennia.

Alongside these, and covered by a fine stalagmitic crust which guarantees their authenticity, many imprints of human feet have been found in the clay. Those from the Ligurian grotto of Toirano are attributed to Neanderthal man,[30] but elsewhere there are footprints of Cro-Magnon man, as well as indefinable traces like those Austrian ones which make us think of unknown races.

At Toirano, and in numerous other caves elsewhere, can be seen, alongside the footprints, the scratch marks of the great plantigrades. The opinion of scholars differs about these clawmarks; some attribute them to the "gymnastics"

Fig. 80

Fig. 81

Fig. 82

Fig. 81. Imprints of human feet in the clay of a Ligurian cave at Toirano; they have been attributed to Neanderthal men.

of the animals after the period of hibernation, others think rather of desperate struggles to free themselves from the hunters' nets which enveloped them. Probably we will never know for certain. We can, however, be sure of one thing; prehistoric man had already made the bear the symbol of that cult which has remained alive among various peoples until our own days. In the Drachenloch, moreover, an astonishing discovery was made, that of a stone kist which, when opened, revealed seven well-preserved skulls of *Ursus spelaeus*, whose age has been calculated at about seventy thousand years.

Why did the occupiers of these caves take such trouble to bury the heads of these animals so carefully? Probably for reasons analogous to those which even today compel certain Finnish-sepaking peoples, such as the Mordvins, the Ostyaks, the Zyryans and the Votyaks, to attribute to the bear honors which would be incomprehensible to us if it were not possible to compare them with other strange customs.

No Tungus will kill a bear without reason. And it is not the strength of the animal which frightens this Siberian people; they maintain that the plantigrade, like man, has a soul. "There is an ancient belief among them," says Ivar Lissner, "that the bear is in communication with the Lord of the Mountains and with the sky. . . . Anyone who is on good terms with bears will seldom be harmed by them. . . .[31]" The ceremony after the death of a bear is most important. Its skeleton is put in a tree or on a high platform. The bodies of men are placed, in order to make their ascent easier!

The Ainu (the aboriginal inhabitants of Japan, now living only in the islands of Sakhalin and Hokkaido), who still practise ritual slaughter of the plantigrades, regard them as "Intermediate between men and gods," the Gilyaks (Sakhalin and around the mouths of the Amur) describe them as "sons of the Moon," and the Lapps regard them as their ancestors.

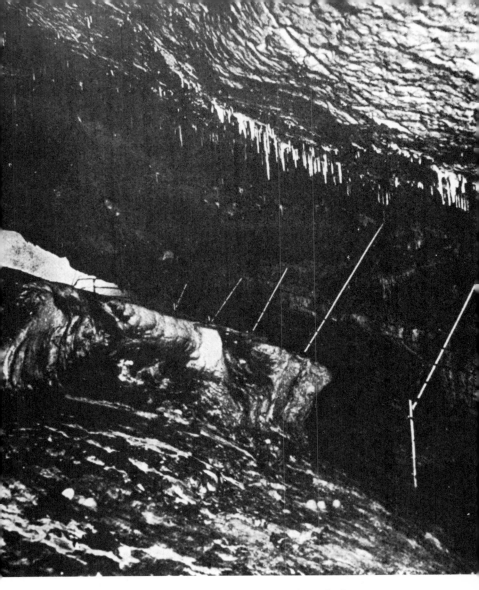

Fig. 82. The feet of men and the paws of gigantic bears
have left traces in the Toirano cave; their authenticity is
guaranteed by the stalagmitic crust which covers them.

115

These common factors are too many to allow us to think of them as mere coincidences. And we shall be even more surprised when we consider that the Iroquois Indians (St. Lawrence, Erie, Ontario) bury their dead wrapped in the skin of a bear, in its turn wrapped in birchbark, whereas the Californian Maidu still today hold a funeral feast where puppets representing those who have died during the past year are shown dressed in bear skins; they are then placed in a circular enclosure and given to the flames "so that they may reach the heavens from which they came!"

It may well be, as Lissner says, that primitive beings have seen "something human" in the gait, the behavior and certain expressions of the bear, but that is not enough to account for the beliefs, the myths, the ceremonies of which we have spoken and which seem to have clear and striking cosmic allusions.

Could there not, moreover, exist a link between the legends of the European, Asian and North American and those of the men "with a double skin" which to some extent flourish in every part of the globe? In other words, couldn't the skin of the plantigrade recall an overall design to protect unknown visitors in a long distant past from atmospheric and climatic conditions alien to them?

"Historians," writes the Soviet academician I. A. Efremov, "must pay more respect to ancient traditions and folklore." He accuses scientists in the West of a certain snobbishness when it comes to the tales of the so-called common people.

And the Frenchman Louis Charpentier: "Today we consider that only the intellectual is civilized. We are no longer able to understand the material traces that remain with us; we have a tendency to consider them the fruit of a certain barbarism and lack of thought. In short, we are unable to escape from our present classifications to search for other and different ones. Yet, without the past civilizations ours would not exist, and we should still be intent upon hunting wild animals and, perhaps, eating one another."

IV

Knights of the Eagles

There are no traces of Pithecanthropos or of Neanderthal man in America. By way of compensation, there is disquieting evidence which clashes with the accepted hypothetical ideas of official science about the inhabitants of "the new world." It tells us of Asian migrations across the Bering Strait. We do not doubt that these migrations took place but, in all probability, they took place only a little before 2000 B.C.

Who, then, are the ancestors of the "white Indians," with fair hair and blue eyes, met with at the beginning of 1969 on the Urubamba at the foot of the Peruvian Andes by the Hamburg explorer, Dietman Carsten? Some have called them descendants of the Vikings who landed in America before Columbus. It is true that the great navigator (as also, later on, the Spanish conquistadores) met similar individuals either in the center or the south of the continent, but if one considers that the first Scandinavian expeditions were towards the middle of the fourteenth century,[32] and, from that time on, the few survivors would have become so merged into the indigenous peoples as to lead to the rapid disappearance of their original traits, one remains perplexed.

Fig. 83

Fig. 84

It is even more perplexing if it can be shown that the "whites of America" look upon us from far more remote times. The mammoth-hunter found by Helmut de Terra in the valley of Mexico doubtlessly perished in the course

Fig. 83. The explorer Carsen with the "white Indians" of Peru.

of an unlucky expedition and almost certainly belonged to our race. Nor can we classify in any other way the very celebrated, bearded Quetzalcoatl whose portrait stands out on a Teotihuacán vase, and the "Palenque man" depicted, also with a beard, just at the spot where a sepulchral slab seems to antedate by who knows how many centuries the history of astronautics. And there is something more to astound us; alongside this portrait stand out the features of an enigmatic face which seems enclosed in a space-helmet!

Nor must we forget the superb Aztec "Knight of the Eagle" whose features speak to us of a race which has very little about it of the "indigenous" (as we understand the expression); and we must bear in mind the cosmic symbolism of this people, for whom the military orders of the Knights of the Eagle and of the Jaguar mirror "the war between day and night." It was just from "the eternal night," from the obscurity of space, that were descended,

Fig. 85

Fig. 86

Fig. 87

Fig. 84. A young wife of the strange tribe settled on the Urubamba with her two very fair offspring.

according to tradition, the "jaguar-men" or "cat-men" of whom, though we have already spoken of them, we shall have occasion to speak again.

The Aztecs made their appearance on the high central plateau of Mexico in the early years of the tenth century. Though many hypotheses have been made, their country

Fig. 85. The bearded Quetzalcoatl on a shard of a Teotihuacán vase.

of origin remains uncertain. They call to mind, however, the mythical Aztlan, the "lost land of the East," which some scholars identify with Atlantis.[33]

"Vatican Codex A-3738," Tomas tells us, "contains a significant chronology of the Aztecs according to which the first cycle continued for 4,008 years ending in a flood. The second of 4,010 years was destroyed by hurricanes. The third era of 4,801 years was closed by fires. In the fourth period which lasted 5,042 years, mankind suffered starvation. The present era is the fifth and it began in 751 B.C. The duration of all four periods listed in this Codex is 17,861 years; and its beginning is traced to an incredibly distant date of 18,612 B.C."[34]

Also, as far as the Maya are concerned, traditional ideas

*Fig. 86. The face of a bearded man beside what might be
a "space mask" from Temple XVIII at Palenque.*

will have to be radically revised. "The Mayan calendar,"
Tomas writes, "shows that the ancient peoples of Central
America had long cycles of 2,760 years. The beginning
of one span is traced to the year 3373 B.C. Three periods
of 2,700 years, or 8,280 years from 3373 B.C., would take
us back to 11,653 B.C. which, within a year, is the same
date as that of the sages of India."

"It is almost certain," confirms Richard Hennig, "that
the Maya traditions record sidereal events going back to
the ninth millennium B.C."[35] And Tomas continues: "Bishop
Diego de Landa wrote in 1566 that in his time the Mayas

Fig. 87. The famous head of the Aztec "Knight of the Eagle."

reckoned their calendar from a date which was about 3113 B.C. in European chronology. They claimed that 5,125 years had passed before this date in former cycles. This would move the origin of the early Mayas to 8,238 B.C., or close to the period of Atlantean cataclysm."

It is interesting to note, while on this subject, how the

Egyptians, with their calculations based on solar cycles of 1,460 years, provide us with a method of stabilizing the beginning of their calendar (starting from the last "astronomical epoch," that is to say from 139 A.D.) at about 11,542 B.C. The Assyrians, for their part, basing their calculations on a lunar calendar divided time into periods of 1,805 years. The last of such periods ended in 712 B.C. and, calculating six lunar cycles, goes back to 11,542 B.C. The Egyptian and Assyrian calendars, therefore, coincide with amazing exactness as far as their origins are concerned!

A goddess in a miniskirt

Certain very ancient races have become prominent and have been extinguished, leaving indications too vague and too meager for us to be able to outline even the most important phases of their history.

Who were the "cat-men" whose enigmatic features appear on so many reproductions and who played their part in so many legends of Central and South America? Perhaps those recorded by the very beautiful skulls carved from solid blocks of crystal, in natural size, by the Miztecs and Aztecs. "It is really amazing," one savant points out, "that these craftsmen succeeded in producing such delicate works with stone tools." But who can assure us that they really used stone tools?

Other races gaze at us from a past closed to us by the proverbial seven seals. These races, very different from one another, are pictured in some of the mysterious ornaments of the "new world": a bearded Maya, the man with the elongated head from Pomona (British Honduras), the face of an unclassifiable Central American being.

Equally indefinable is the so-called "Xipe Totec"; he should be an Aztec divinity but his features are such that some scholars have hinted at a cross between the Indians and the famous "cat-men."

We find this last also in the sinister Easter Island carvings:

Fig. 88

Fig. 89

Fig. 90

Fig. 91

Fig. 92 a bearded figure with long earrings; a strange woman bearing a fish on her shoulders; and a figure which seems to be a whale with a cabin of reeds upon its back. If this is so, then these marine carvings might refer to a record of the Deluge in one of its two known versions.

Nor is this all: in 1971, once again thanks to the enthusiastic work of Mario Salomone, a "great mask" carved in the rock which closely recalls certan primitive South American portrayals of the "creatures with flat heads" was *Fig. 93* discovered in Piedmont (Villarfocchiardo, Valle di Susa). Any affinity between them is, even if not arbitrary, certainly rash. Nonetheless, we must achknowledge that this find by the Turin archaeologist is the only European example which recalls the transoceanic finds.

Pure coincidence? Perhaps. But archaeology is too rich in such "coincidences" for them not to be significant. The strange humanoid head found in China, of the Han period (from 206 B.C. to 25 A.D.), for example, puts us in mind of *Fig. 94* many Polynesian wood carvings which mirror the deeds of "the gods with two heads who came out of the fire." We do not know what was meant by the "fire," though some scholars hint at possible mutations which took place in the most remote times, as a result of cataclysms which could have led, among other thing, to tremendous volcanic eruptions. It is in any case remarkable that the Chinese figure has two large protuberances on its forehead.

Fig. 95 On the "Lion Gate" of Boghazköy in central Anatolia, among the strange sculptures, which archaeologists tell us antedate by several centuries the similar works on Assyrian buildings we can still admire the stone heads which, though *Fig. 96* ravaged by time and weather, recall more or less closely the mysterious monuments of Easter Island.

Quite Sybilline, on the other hand, seems to us the so-called "Mother-goddess" of Mohenjo-Daro, the center of an unknown civilization which came to light on what today is a tiny island in the Indus river, southwest of Skkur in Pakistan.

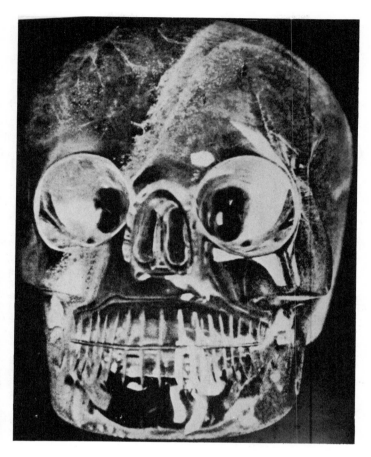

Fig. 88. A very beautiful skull made of crystal, probably
of Mixtec origin; its features recall those of the cat-men.

For the most notable characteristics of its ruins, let us
quote from what was said in *Timeless Earth*:

"Its most impressive building is a bath-house, formerly
covered, with a pool measuring 40 feet by 23 feet; alongside it is a steam-bath and a hot-air heating system. The

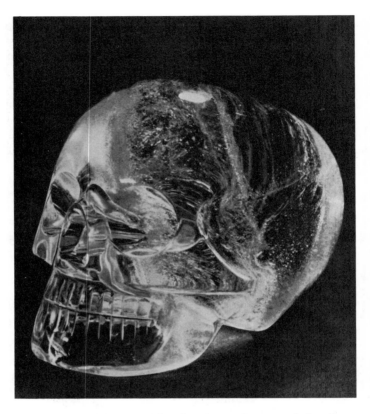

Fig. 89. A skull carved by the Aztecs in natural size from a single block of crystal.

main street, running north and south, is over half a mile long and 33 feet wide. The houses were of one or two stories or sometimes three, and were expertly built in brick similar to ours. Each bedroom had running water and a bathroom and lavatory; this, as the plumbing system shows, was also true of the upper floors, now destroyed. The municipal sewerage was so efficient that British engineers declared they could do no better at the present day."

Fig. 90. (Above) A Maya pendant representing a bearded man. (Center, left) An earring from Pomona (British Honduras). (Below, right) A Central American mask of unidentifiable type.

Perfectly in line with this "modernity" is the statuette to which we have alluded, a woman in the most daring of miniskirts and a necklace and belt which would arouse the   *Fig. 97*

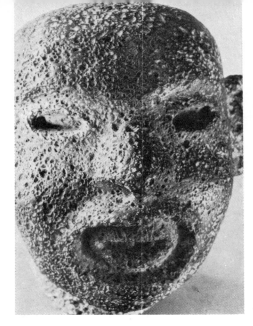

Fig. 91. An Aztec
stone model of the
god Xipe Totec.
Racially, it seems to
be unidentifiable.

Fig. 92. Some strange carvings of the late Easter Island
period; above, a bearded being with long earrings and a
"whale with a reed cabin on its back"; below, a strange
skull and a "woman with a fish on her back."

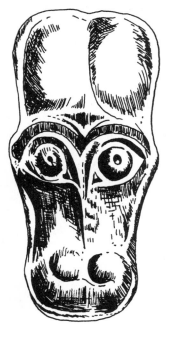

Fig. 93. The bizarre "great mask" discovered by Mario Salomone near Villarfocchiardo in the Valle di Susa (Piedmont) recalls, by bizarre coincidence, the extinct American flat-skulled race.

Fig. 94. A Chinese ornament of the Han Period (206 B.C.-25 A.D.) calls to mind the "two-headed god who came out of the fire."

envy of a girl of our own days. Two things, however, are not in harmony with the picture we are tempted to outline: the head-covering, of inexplicable structure for many reasons, and the features of the girl herself, which we certainly cannot consider attractive.

Fig. 98 Nor are the features of the figurines found in the vicinity of Mexico City (once again these photos are by courtesy of Robert Calcagno) very attractive from our point of view. They represent little men, some with almost perfectly oval heads, others with a cranium which, greatly elongated, tapers off as if they were wearing fezzes (there is, however, no trace of a head-covering), and still others with protuberances on the back of the head.

Such characteristics make us think of the cranial deformations practised in various parts of the world, from Central Africa to the New Hebrides, from Indonesia and Polynesia to western America. These figurines, however, Fig. 99 come from the Olmec culture, to which such deformations were alien. And not only this: it was this civilization which left to us the most remarkable monumental heads of the "cat-men." [36]

It is worth noting that these figurines are variously colored; some are green, some red, some white and, setting aside the question of the deformations themselves, their features seem to mirror all existing races, and also some which we are unable to classify.

Fig. 100 Another detail which strikes us is the presence of obelisks alongside the figurines. We must not forget that the Olmecs knew the stele and attributed to it (insofar as we know

Fig. 95. (Opposite page, above) The inexplicable sculptures of the Lion Gate of Boghazköy not only anticipate the anologous works of the Assyrians but also recall the features of the Easter Island statues.

Fig. 96. (Opposite page, below) Two "stone giants" on Easter Island.

Fig. 97. The "goddess in a miniskirt" from Mohenjo-Daro.

anything of their traditions, reported by other peoples) a significance which allied it to the cosmos; the civilizations which developed under Olmec influence speak of such monoliths as "lances" (or "points") intended to "transfix the skies."

Were the ancient inhabitants of the countries around the Gulf of Mexico, who arrived there by who knows what route and were at one time ruled by a "very powerful magician," the custodians of "forgotten sciences"? And did they preserve cosmic records of which we have no idea? Or did they receive their astonishing ideas directly from the astronauts of prehistory? There are some who do not hesitate to say so.

Accustomed as we are to define the pre-Columbian Americans as "redskins" (which is only partially true), it could be of interest to look at the primitive obelisks, roughly two and a half meters high (they are divided into

Fig. 98. Strange nightmare figures found near Mexico City.

Fig. 99. These Mexican statuettes, attributed to the Olmec culture, are diversely colored, in red, green and white. Their features seem to mirror all the races in existence, as well as others totally unidentifiable.

Fig. 100. A strange detail is the presence of small cylindrical columns among the statuettes of presumed Olmec origin. Is it an allusion to the cosmos? The traditions speak of "lances designed to pierce the skies."

Fig. 101. A New Zealand totem pole, remarkably similar to those found in North America.

Fig. 102. Strange "non-native" faces carved on a totem pole of the Haida Indians of the northwest coast of North America.

135

two groups, one of a hundred and fifty, the other about fifty) which can be seen in a district called Toundinaro, sixteen kilometers (25.6 mi.) from Niafounke on the Niger. The natives say that they were erected by the Bagara, lengendary "red men" who ruled this part of the country in the past, as has been shown by finds of human remains, "together with different races who lived in a very remote past." [37]

"One finds 'redskins,' " Charpentier points out, "not only in America but also in the eastern Mediterranean. We see the Ghomara (the 'Reds') in the neighborhood of the holy city of Chaouen in the Riff. The word 'Phoenician' means *red* and the Phoenicians occupied, as well as the shores of the Red Sea, the whole coast of the Asian Near East and numerous islands such as Crete. We note that the Egyptians called the Cretans *Keftin* and pictured them as beardless with red skins, precisely like the Phoenicians themselves." [38]

While still on the subject of columnar monuments, let us devote a few words to totem poles. From Oceania to America, among faces of familiar appearance, we can discern the features of distant, sometimes unknown, races. The multiplicity of expressions leaves us stunned, as for

Fig. 101

example on a totem pole of the Haida, the Amerindians of Queen Charlotte Island (western Canada). It is surmounted by a strange animal figure intended to represent the "god come from the sky," "the great master of all men," of those, that is, pictured on the totem itself, from whom the

Fig. 102

Haida were separated by unimaginable distances and of whose existence they should, logically, have been quite unaware.

The monster from the cold

In the beginning were the monkeys. Not quite at the beginning, but near enough. Even earlier there appeared on the earth beings which "crawled on all-fours aimlessly" and were exterminated: "The Heart of the Sky caused a deluge and great waters fell . . . liquid resin poured from the skies, the face of the Earth was darkened and a black rain poured down, by day and by night. . . ."

Thus the *Popol Vuh*, explaining the fate of these creatures: "It is said that their descendants are the monkeys which live today in the forests. In these can be recognized those whose flesh was made of wood by the Creator. For that reason the monkeys resemble man, the memory of a human creation when men were no more than wooden puppets." [39]

The "Maya bible" thus summarizes, in the form of a legend, the story of evolution and of the castrophes which devastated our planet. A synthesis is offered us in an illustration in the *Vatican Codex A6* which shows us Quetzal-coatl as the creative divinity surrounded by amorphous beings, monkeys, animals, trees, turned towards a definitely human couple, the completion of his task. *Fig. 103*

The story of the "monkey-men" is alive not only in America, but also in various African regions. The Baule *Fig. 104* of the Ivory Coast preserve to this day a very evocative image, that of Mbotumbo who (and the fact seems to us significant) is not really a god but a sort of divinity of lower rank, a kind of chief of the monkeys, if one may so call him.

"In Thrace and in northern Greece," we read in an interesting study by Gaster, "it is the custom to celebrate certain important festivals with a crude pantomime, and an essential feature of the spectacle is the unexpected intrusion, during a wedding feast, of a vociferous oaf in a black mask who tries to molest the bride and lays hands on the bridegroom. In Thessaly this person is usually represented as a savage and hiry 'Arab' and, the better to stress his barbarian character, he wears in addition to the black mask of sheep- or goat-skin, a sheepskin coat and sometimes also a tail." [40]

Many factors make us think of the existence of simian beings more or less allied to man, as we know him, but not such as to represent the famous "missing link" so long sought after.

Towards the end of 1969, some scholarly traditionalist thought that he had found this missing link and was in seventh heaven. A very strange creature had been fished up in the Bering Sea, frozen in an ice floe. The story of this creature is wrapped in mystery. There are those who say that it came from a shipwrecked Japanese ship and others who provide an alternative version.

Fig. 105 "Bozo" (the "monster who came in from the cold" was thus baptized) was found quite by chance by the crew of a Soviet sealer. When the ship arrived at a Chinese port, the strange find was sent to Hong Kong and there handed over to the members of an American scientific institution.

We have not been allowed to know which scientific institution; the whole episode is enveloped in absolute secrecy. That "Bozo" is not a figment of the imagination is, however, certain: the United States journalist Ivan T. Sanderson has photographed it; the zoologist Heuvelmanns, member of the Brussels Academy of Sciences, has been able to study it at close range, after having pledged himself and many of his colleagues to keep secret the place where it was kept.

Fig. 106 "Bozo," the so-called *Homo Pongoides*, is a creature about 1.80 meters (6 ft.) tall, muscular, almost devoid of neck, with long arms and spatulate hands. Its feet are 25 centimeters (10 in.) long and, except for its face, the palms of its hands and the soles of its feet, it is covered with hair up to about ten centimeters (0.4 in.) long. It must have died from a head wound. But when could this being have lived? "Up until about five years ago," declared Heuvelmanns, and added that the resemblance to the famous yeti, as it has been described by eyewitnesses, is more than noteworthy; it is striking.

Tarzan and the monkey-woman

So not even the "living fossils" allied to our own species

Fig. 103. (Left) The Vatican Codex A.6 shows us Quet-zalcoatl as divine creator surrounded by amorphous be-ings, monkeys, various animals and trees, but looking towards a definitely human couple.

Fig. 104. (Right) Mbotumbo, the "monkey-god" of the Baule people of the Ivory Coast.

are dead? It really seems not. Every so often, on the other hand, beings which appear to show that traditional theories on evolution must be, as we have already said, radically revised and corrected make a "final appearance." The "abominable snowman" is, if we may so express it, of yesterday. But today there is a creature even closer to us in appearance but, at the same time, so alien to us as to make us shudder.

Do you remember *The Planet of the Apes*, that science-fiction film based on an equally well-known story, which shows us very evolved, knowledgeable and civilized pri-mates? Could you imagine a monkey-woman of the screen translated into reality? We had not been able to go so far,

Fig. 107

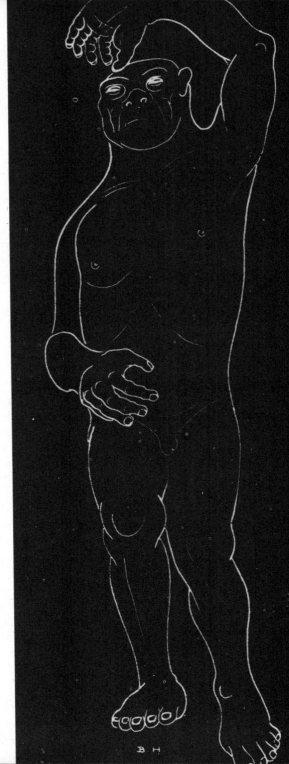

Fig. 105. (Opposite page) The "monster who came from the cold," fished up in the Bering Sea enclosed in a block of ice. On the right the original photograph and on the left a reconstruction.

Fig. 106. Outline of the Homo Pongoides *from a scientific periodical.*

Fig. *108*

but we have now had to surrender to the evidence of the being discovered in an isolated village in the forest in the Brazilian state of Minas Gerais.[41]

It is a being which certainly does not possess the intelligence of the quadromanes of the film but which, on the other hand, is much closer in appearance to its "man cousins." It is thirteen years old and female; its eyes are large and protuberant, its nose flat, its mouth wide, its jaw

Fig. *109*

in every way similar to that of a chimpanzee; its body is covered with black hair, very thick on the back and spine.

The local inhabitants call the girl Maria de Jesus, perhaps out of pity, but certainly that name underlines the horrifying aspect of the story. Who were the parents of this thirteen-year-old? Nobody knows and nobody has taken the trouble to find out. The state of misery in which these people live is enough to prevent them looking farther than the immediate past.

An ethnologist unexpectedly turned up in the village, saw the unfortunate creature and promised her that he would return. When speaking of her, he aroused the interest of other scholars who organized a full-scale expedition, forcing their way through the jungle with machetes, as far as the village without a name, only visited every so often by missionaries bringing cast-off clothing, food and such medicines as they managed to glean.

What has science to say about poor Maria de Jesus? Let us hear from the professor of pathology, Joao Henrique de Freitas Filhos:

"All human beings have animal traits. It is not improbable that the girl may have had ancestors who were, let us say, 'bizarre' and who lived perhaps many centuries ago.

"Today we know that the animal traits alluded to are even more evident in the embryonic phase of life; the new individual has, in its mother's womb, hair like monkeys and scales like fishes. But as a general, almost universal, rule such peculiarities disappear about the third month of gestation. The phenomenon is known as *phylogenesis* or 'evolu-

Fig. 107. The "mutant" from the film The Planet of the Apes.

tion of the species,' but at the same time there develops the phenomenon of *ontogenesis* or 'formation of the being,' in the course of which the baby acquires, for example, the blue eyes of its father or a nose similar in shape to its mother's.

"The two processes are well synchronized; in the present state of our knowledge it is considered that they cannot be

Fig. 108. The real "monkey-woman" discovered in the Brazilian state of Minas Gerais.

Fig. 109. (Opposite page) Another striking picture of the "monkey-woman"; a sort of thick mane flows down her spine.

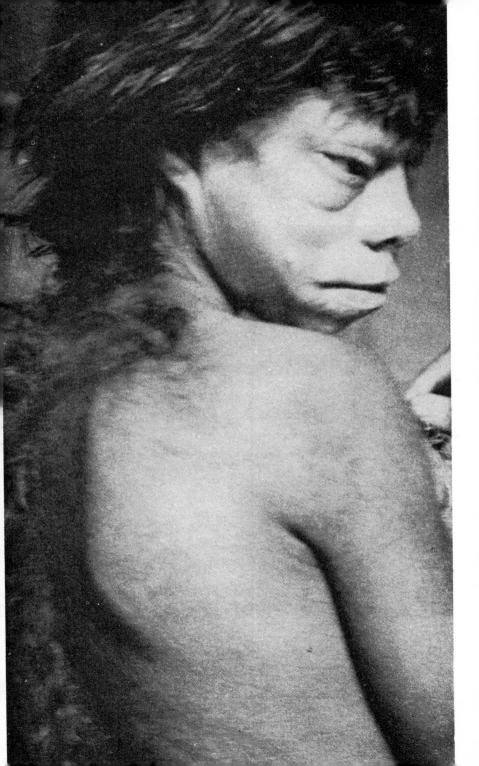

dissociated. It is, thanks to them, that one may sometimes resemble neither father nor mother, but some ancestor.

"In colloquial language, one can 'jump' one or two generations, rarely more. The case of Maria is therefore astounding."

There is another astonishing fact; at birth the unhappy creature was, in appearance, like any other baby. She acquired, little by little, the simian traits which thenceforth marked her. "One must therefore think of some divergence of the genetic make-up, something without precedent."

Maria de Jesus cannot speak and appears stupid. She is docile, tame as a domestic animal, but possesses a marked sensitivity. She runs away, terrified, when the village children shout rude names at her. Often she goes away alone and weeps for a long time. Why? She cannot say why and others cannot guess.

The scholars, who have in the meantime confided her to the care of a local family, are thinking of transferring her to a hospital in some great city in order to examine her thoroughly.

Science has therefore accomplished something. Maria will be freed from hunger and derision. But what will her reactions be when faced with civilization? And what will her future be when all the research is over?

We certainly cannot be too optimistic about this, especially when we consider the attitude of the Brazilian authorities towards the Indians.

Totally primitive beings, unknown humanoids, monkey-women, descendants of the Neanderthals, yeti: creatures such as these live alongside us, arousing the most fantastic conjectures of our civilization. They are far too numerous to allow us to speak of "freaks of nature." To those so far reported we can add very many other examples; and they lead us to think that we are faced with real "living fossils," representatives of races almost completely wiped off the face of the globe by apocalyptic events.

The *Popol Vuh* tells us, in easily interpreted expressions, of floods, meteoric showers and volcanic eruptions which overwhelmed the earth, leaving only tiny islands of life. Similar descriptions are met with in very many legends from every part of the world.

What is it that happens so suddenly to species which have become extinct? Some researchers are trying to work out an answer in more scientific terms as, for that matter, we have already done in other volumes of this collection.

"We are asked, for example," we read in the Milanese weekly L'Europeo,[42] "why some very small marine organisms, already much diffused, became extinct within a period which, in relation to the geological time scale, may be considered as short. This phenomenon has been verified many times and has affected different varieties of plankton in the last four million years.

"However, there is an important clue. *Some of these extinctions seem to have taken place at the precise moment when the earth's magnetic field was changing, in such a manner that the north magnetic pole became the south magnetic pole, and vice versa. From a study of magnetism carried out on rocks, geologists know that the magnetic field has been turned inside out at least twenty times in course of the last four million years and very many other times in the ages before then.*

"One theory is that, halfway through this change, the terrestial magnetic field must have diminished to zero. *The cosmic radiation, which normally deviates from the earth along the lines of force, could then have penetrated to the surface of the earth, giving rise to mutations which in the end led to the extinction of many species.*"

Another point of view, which Professor J. P. Kennet and Dr. N. D. Wilkins of the University of Rhode Island have tried to prove in researches recently published, is that *the extinctions were due to volcanic paroxysms taking place contemporaneously with changes in the magnetic field.* The two scientists make use of the arguments put forward in 1968 by James Heirtzler of the Geological

Observatory of Lamont, New York, according to which a *period of violent volcanic activity could have reversed the rotation of the earth.*

"They have tried to show that the outburst of volcanic activity took place during the reversal of the earth's magnetic field by examining the fossil sediments found in the Pacific, in southeast New Zealand, measuring the direction of the magnetism within the sediments themselves and searching for strata of volcanic dust. In many cases signs of volcanic activity corresponding to the reversal of the magnetic field were found, and the scientists maintain that it is difficult to believe that this is due to casual coincidence."

It is certain that, as a result of such phenomena, not only various types of plankton became extinct but also, and far more easily, many forms of more highly developed life.

They even have the courage to speak of the human species, to confront the demand which has so often been made: "If, alongside these primitive species which must have left some survivors, there lived on Earth some highly intelligent beings, why is it that they have left as their heritage to the ancient cultures only a few pale memories of their presumed great achievements?"

We reply with an elementary example: if it so happened that we were able to save our lives after an air-crash in the dense jungle and were able to salvage from the debris of the plane whatever remained intact or nearly so, which might be of use to us, we should go on living for some time with an appearance of civilization. But only for a time: the batteries of the lighting plant and the radio would become exhausted, the metals become oxidized. Our improvised dwelling would fall to pieces and our clothing be reduced to rags and tatters. We should be able to communicate a few basic ideas to the natives among whom we had fallen but we should have to adapt ourselves in the end to their way of life. We should have to do so without delay as is proven by the last example in order of time—the story of Tarzan.

148

Dawn was breaking in the Amazon forest when the camp sentinels heard the guttural cry from the tangle of trees, lianas, undergrowth and gigantic flowers.

The men on guard reacted immediately, while the members of the expedition, led by Professor Francisco Meirelles, leaped to their feet and rushed for their weapons. Another couple of minutes and it would have been too late; a horde of naked Indians, wielding knives and stone axes, suddenly fell upon the camp. The Brazilians responded with a furious volley and the aggressors withdrew, leaving some dead and wounded in the clearing, upon which rained down from a distance clouds of poisoned arrows.

Calm was returning to the camp, when an angry voice was raised:

"Do you know who brought the Indians upon us? It was one of us, Silvio! He had taken off his jacket but I recognized him. It was he who was leading them!"

The men of the expedition turned threateningly on Silvio, one of Meirelles' assistants.

"Have you gone mad?" retorted the so-called traitor, "What do you take me for? Why should I have done such a thing?"

His protests poured oil on the waters, but were no longer heeded when there was another attack on the camp a day or so later. Some of the men swore that they had seen Silvio quite clearly among the Indians and the professor had to intervene energetically to prevent a lynching.

The matter did not end there. A group of whites and half-breeds decided to put an end to it once and for all and assassinate the suspected colleague. He, seriously wounded, escaped by a miracle and had to be sent back by helicopter.

After that the Brazilians were left in peace. It seemed an unimpeachable proof of Silvio's guilt, but Professor Meirelles was not convinced. On his way back he fell in with a group of white hunters who had for years hunted in those parts, told them what had happened and got the prompt reply:

"Oh, we know something of that. The guy leading the

Indians was Tarzan, the white chief of the Mekronotire."
Only too often had the savant heard of the legendary white leader. Only too often, searching for him, he had only come across natives of a pale color. Surprising, yes, for their features were similar to ours, but not so similar as to astonish the expert scientist. Tarzan, then. . .

"It is only a nickname we have given him," the hunters explained. "We don't know what his name is, but we don't advise you to go and ask him in person. He is a ruthless devil!"

That happened about ten years ago. Meirelles, however, did not follow this advice; with a fresh expedition he penetrated as far as the Rio Chinche, found the Mekronotire tribe and met Silvio's double.

Fig. 110 It was "Tarzan."

Certainly he did not greatly resemble Johnny Weissmuller who was the most famous "king of the jungle" on the screen, nor any of his innumerable successors and imitators. He was very thin, all muscles and nerve, freckled, with brown hair with a tinge of red in it. He was indubitably a white man, even though he did not understand a word of Portuguese, and was called Bemontire, in the local dialect "Wild Beast."

A warrior? He was more than a warrior; he was the chief of the Mekronotire, one of the most primitive and ferocious races of the Brazilian jungle which had come down from the Rio Xingu and for generations had dominated the territory between the Rio Iriri and the Rio Chinche.

"I come in peace," Meirelles said.

The other looked at him suspiciously, remaining for some time on his guard. In the end he was convinced that the white man really did not have evil intentions. Thus

Fig. 110. (Opposite page) They call him Tarzan; he is the white chief of the tribe of bellicose Makronotire Amazon Indians.

the professor and the tribal chief became friends. And the chief told the scholar his story, as he had heard it from the elders of his tribe.

"In May 1930 our warriors attacked fifteen rubbergatherers who, with their families, had settled in our territory, preventing us from hunting and fishing, and refusing to go away. The whites were all killed except for a child about two years old. He was taken away by a warrior who adopted him and brought him up as all little Indians are brought up. I was that baby. . ."

Naturally, we have not translated the account word by word, but have condensed the story told by Bemontire to Meirelles in one of the many dialects that the professor knew. The word "ours," however, occurs again and again in the original version; the chief considered himself an Indian through and through, even though he knew that he was born a white (Dutch, as was afterwards established). As far back as he could remember, he had hated the "pale skins." But now he had become convinced by certain experiences that he should stop killing them, though he went on killing members of other indigenous races who laid ambushes for his people.

Bemontire's story was filled with struggle. His adoptive father pierced his ears, according to custom, in order to insert the ritual sticks and fixed in his lower lip the wooden disc intended to give a terrifying appearance to the warriors. He had also instructed him in the use of the axe and stone knives and the bow and the boy soon became so skilled in their use that he was recognized as a war leader undisputed by his equals in years.

When we reached the age of virility, the tribal chief offered him his daughter Opodikoi in marriage. It was a great honor and Bemontire showed himself worthy of it, leading the warriors against the enemy with incredible courage. His companion bore him two sons (Karotka and Bepre) and two daughters (Ireo and Kereri) and our Tarzan lived with the Mekronotire according to their laws,

Fig. 111

152

Fig. 111. Bemontire and his family. From the left: his wife Opodikoi and his sons Karotka and Bepre, Tarzan himself and his daughter Kereri.

becoming their chief on the death of his father-in-law.

With his "record" and the brutal war of extermination waged against the Indians by the present Brazilian government, it would have turned out pretty badly for him if he had not in the meantime encountered Professor Meirelles. Having fallen on a watch fire after an attack of malaria, Bemontire received burns which later turned septic.

Some scholars from UNESCO found him almost dying. They treated him as well as they could with antibiotics and wanted to take him to a hospital in Brazilia. The "white Indian," however, energetically refused. One of his rescuers, however, recognized him and advised Meirelles who rushed to the spot and persuaded the chief to let himself be healed.

In Brazilia the daring war-leader behaved like a frightened rabbit. Already terrorized by the aerial voyage, pushed forcibly into a car, he gripped the professor's arm with one hand and covered his eyes with the other. Meirelles sweated out seven shirts before he could induce him to remain quietly in the hospital. Day and night an Indian who knew his language and had worked for some time alongside the white scientists sat at the end of the warrior's bed.

After his recovery Bemontire learned how to wear clothes and how to enjoy the pleasures of the city. Not all, however: he absolutely refused to remain seated before the television, detested crowded and enclosed places and refused to eat the food of the "palefaces" (except their sweets, which he ate gluttonously). He continually asked for maize, bananas and "pure water." He was quite indifferent to gifts; he felt only the desire to leave. Even in the course of two subsequent visits to the Brazilia garrison he did nothing but insist that he be taken back as soon as possible to his own land.

His? Yes, definitely his!

It is a story which would be equally applicable to our own race and to the planet on which we live today if its representatives had been saved millennia ago from the drowning of Atlantis or from the disastrous end of some expedition which came from Alpha Centauri.

V

Stellar Missions

Proofs of the existence of forms of life on other planets
rain down continually on Earth and not in a figurative
sense. Strange radio messages, even though indecipherable,
are received more and more frequently (the most recent,
even as we are writing, come from that enigmatic region
of the Pleiades, to which so many legends refer, indications
of a very remote past). Meteorites, without doubt containing organic substances, are continually falling on our earth.

Not so long ago another "missile from the Universe"
provided us with irrefutable proof, should we have needed
it, that life is not a phenomenon conceded uniquely to our
planet. This was the meteorite which fell in the vicinity
of Murchison in Australia on September 28, 1969. Thanks
to the work of Dr. Cyril Ponnamperuma, head of the
analysis department of the NASA Space Research Center
at Mountain View in California, twenty types of amino-
acids present in the living cells of our planet, together with
eleven others whose structure is unknown to us, were discovered by the end of 1970.

But how are we to picture our "Brothers of the Infinite"? More or less like ourselves, say the German geolo-
gist Bernhardt Rensch and the American anthropologist
William Howells, supporters of the theory of "parallel
evolution" who assert that life can only originate where
there is carbon as a means of forming hydrocarbons. But,
together with several Soviet scientists, Eiseley, another

Fig. 112

Fig. 113

Fig. 112. Radio signals reach us today from the Pleiades, a constellation which strangely enough recurs often in the stellar myths. In this fragment of an ancient Mesopotamian calendar we see them pictured on the left, together with a god or a hero enclosed in a circle, and the Bull.

Fig. 113. The Murchison meteorite (called after the place in Australia where it was found); various types of amino acids have been found in it, a final proof that life is not an exclusive prerogative of Earth.

American anthropologist, replies that life need not necessarily be linked either to the structures already known to us or to the "oxygenated world," as is demonstrated in striking fashion by the Earth itself.[43]

Strictly logically, one theory need not exclude the other. What is there to tell us that if our planet has welcomed visitors from space in the past, its guests may not have differed greatly among themselves? And who is there to assure us that becaue they are not mirrored in the fantasies of science fiction, however daring, they were not derived from life upon the Earth in one of its multiple forms, sometimes incomprehensible?

Expedition from Rigel

It was some kind of huge shell, enveloped in orange fire. It plummeted from space into the night sky of Earth at a fantastic velocity, suddenly stopped, and wavered.

Then came the catastrophe. A very luminous ball of fire fell heavily to earth, followed by a wake of greenish, yellowish, blue gas. The pilot of the space vehicle clenched his teeth, trying to control the course of the spaceship. Then the Sun rotated before his eyes, the globe exploded in a thousand outbursts, with all its volcanoes aflame and immense clouds rose upward to the skies.

"Pilot to crew, pilot to crew!" the voice of the cosmonaut announced over the microphone. "We have arrived too late. The natural satellite of the third planet of this system has just fallen, a short time ago. Everyone to his post. Put all safety measures into operation. I am trying for a forced landing."

The great shell was tossed up and down, caught in a whirlwind, and seemed as if it would be smashed down to earth. Then, at the critical moment, the final convulsion. The vehicle skimmed over the crest of a hill and fell on to a rocky tableland.

"Close the compartment doors," the pilot shouted over the radio. "No one is to go out until the atmosphere outside is breathable."

He unlaced his flying suit and threw down the gloves angrily on the instrument panel. The small door of the control room opened and a woman entered, the biologist of the expedition.

"How are the crew taking it?" the man asked.

"A bruise or two, but nothing serious. You got out of that very well. And the spaceship?"

"Done for," the other answered laconically. "Completely done for. We haven't the slightest chance of leaving this planet."

"We shall begin again from the beginning," the woman replied; and added something which if we could translate it according to our ideas would be "Adam and Eve."

This episode is obviously the fruit of our fantasy. Keeping in mind, however, all that we have said in the previous chapter, we could consider the hypothesis (which is finding an ever growing number of defenders) according to which the first men were not born on Earth, but fell by chance upon this earth from who knows what world

We do not want to become adherents of this theory unreservedly. Let us admit, however, that its supporters have given us something to unleash our imagination, recalling the Creation myths which say that humanity was born from an egg, from a not very well defined mollusk or from a tortoise.

It seems superfluous for us to repeat the story of the "cosmogonic egg." Let us add only the references of Vedic India to the mollusk, enclosing the demiurge, the possible links with the Assyro-Babylonian and Etruscan traditions, and the close identification of the "egg" itself with the shell of a legendary turtle which is to be found among very many peoples of northern, central and southern America.

Among the Hurons of the north, "the world originated from a woman, Ataentsic, who fell from Heaven upon the back of a turtle which floated upon the waters. The muskrat dived to the bottom of the waters, took up a little mud and formed the earth upon which Ataentsic gave birth to the twins Ioskcha and Tawiskara or, according to another version, Manobozho and Chokanipola." [44]

Let us move on a little and listen to how the Canadian Athabascans tell the same legend of Creation. Alone, the mother of the twins fell into the shell of an egg (that of the "great Crow," that is to say, a flying being) which was the origin of the tortoise. For the Puelce of austral America, however, the egg floated on the primordial waters and began to move thanks to rowers which suddenly appeared and from the shell came forth twins, male and female, to whom the human race owes it existence!

Doesn't it seem that we are faced with the story of a space shipwreck translated into fable?

The Arapaho of Wyoming and Oklahoma also attribute the Creation of a tortoise "aided by a bird." It is from this reptile that the classical Chinese dragon is born and a great stone tortoise of probably cosmic signficance is all that remains of Karakorum, the Mongol capital, founded by Ogultai, the son of Genghis Khan.

In Madagascar personages of royal blood, direct descendants of the gods, are reincarnated as tortoises according to a widely diffused Malagasy belief, and the same happens to the chiefs of the Bushmen, who live in hemispherical huts and whose women wear, as talismans, boxes made from the shell of the reptile, containing powdered, perfumed wood.

Today the tortoise is still a cosmogonic symbol among the aborigines of Arnhem Land (already mentioned for their pictures of serpents) who depict it on the bark of trees.

Fig. 114

The schematic designs of the shell of a tortoise are similar to the carvings photographed at Rabat by the explorer Willy Fassio; archaeologists consider them to be solar symbols or rudimentary calendars but it seems to us that their link with the local legends, referring to "round stones fallen from the sky," should not be overlooked,

Fig. 115

Fig. 116

the more so as we find very similar graffiti at the Bicknell Museum in Bordighera, which comes from the Valley of Marvels on the Italo-French frontier.

It is not a new hypothesis that before its present satellite the Earth has had other moons which have fallen according to an astronomical law which, in the opinion of some scholars, will also condemn, after some millions of years, our present satellite.[45]

It is probable that eclipses of the Sun or Moon have recalled, and still recall, among various peoples the obscure, ancestral memory of cosmic catastrophes, marked by the disappearance of some heavenly body in orbit around our own planet and the temporary disappearance, due to the consequences of those cataclysms, of the star which gives us life.

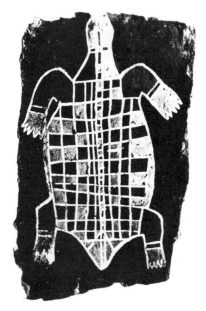

Fig. 114. The "cosmogonic tortoise" of Arnhem Land, a symbol found in many parts of the world.

Fig. 115. Strange rock drawings photographed by Willy
Fassio; scholars believe that they are solar signs or calendars, but their relationship with the legendary "round
stones fallen from the skies" should not be overlooked.

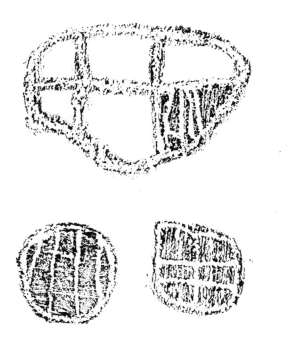

Fig. 116. Graffiti very similar to those found in Morocco can be admired in the Bicknell Museum at Bordighera. They were found in the Valley of Marvels.

The legend of Baal, god of the Canaanites, reflects "the ancient belief that eclipses of the sun and moon were due to the ravages of a celestial dragon which pursued them and devoured them. Thus, according to Indian belief, the dragon Rahu, or Svarbahnu, periodically swallows them. And in a Confucian text, the *Tsun Tsiu* (*Springs and Autumns*), the word eat is used to describe the eclipses of April 20, 610 B.C. In a similar way in various Scandinavian legends the sun is constantly menaced by a wolf called Skoll, whereas in Tatar legends the sun and moon art treacherously attacked by a demon or by the king of hell, and in Hebrew legends by a fish." [46]

Regarding eclipses as the death of the Sun or Moon, the Ojibway redskins, as soon as the phenomenon is observed, loose fiery arrows into the sky in order to rekindle the stars. The Kamchadales light fires outside their huts for the same purpose, whereas the Chilcotin Indians dress in travelling clothes and set out on a sort of propitiatory march, which reflects the exhausting migrations made by their ancestors in the wake of terrible cataclysms. "The so-called 'St. John's fires' which are lit in the form of crowns or braziers at the summer solstice," writes Nicola Turchi, "are intended to reinforce the sun's energy, which begins to diminish after June 21, and the offering of the hearts of youths ceremonially sacrificed by the Aztecs of ancient Mexico to the Sun had the same aim of renewing its forces of warmth and movement. In a similar way should be interpreted the sacrifice of a quadriga which the Rhodians made to the Sun, submerging it in the sea, as well as the offering of horses which the Spartans made to the Sun on Taygetos, behind which the sun sets. It is superfluous to mention the many examples concerning the Moon . . ." [47]

If we accept that astronauts coming from "oxygenated worlds" reached the earth at just the time when these catastrophes to which we have alluded took place, and had to remain there, they must have undergone processes of transformation and adaptation of which we have not the faintest idea.

Let us use our imagination and look at those pictures which many peoples consider to have been of their most distant ancestors; at the beings which, reproduced on certain ceramics in the Nasca style of southern Peru, seem *Fig. 117* destined for amphibious life, at the enigmatic "Tlatilco head" molded on a vase of the pre-classical Mexican *Fig. 118* period, at the mask of the Kuskowogmint shamans of Alaska. The upper circle seems to hint at a headcovering *Fig. 119* (a helmet?), the feathers and the lateral projections certainly express the concept of flight, but the face has an

Fig. 117. These creatures, depicted on a ceramic of the Nasca style (southern Peru), seem destined for an amphibious life.

expression which only distantly recalls that of a human being.

Fig. 120 The same could be said of certain representations of the "Martian period" of the Tassili, so called because the heads of some of the figures seem concealed by space-helmets.

But what can we discern in the drawings of the "divinities" of huge stature which tower above the individuals surrounding them, caught in the act of obvious adoration?

Perhaps they were depicted as giants as a sign of veneration, or perhaps they really were Titans?

Here, once again, the question is posed of the existence on our globe, in the remote past, of gigantic creatures, rendered thus precisely by the phenomena consequent

Fig. 118. The enigmatic "Tlatilco head" molded on a vase of pre-classical Mexico.

upon the fall of earlier satellites. The argument has already been treated in *Timeless Earth* and *Not of this World*, but it does not seem to us out of place to offer further evidence in this matter.

The revolt of the giants

"Of all the stars of the firmament," writes Theodor Gaster in his book already cited in this chapter, "few are more brilliant or make a greater impact on the imagination than those which today form the constellation of Orion. It was therefore natural that our ancestors liked to see in them a portrait especially well known and much revered. . . . This constellation represented the Great Hunter, the tallest, the strongest and the most beautiful of all men, he who dared to insult the goddess of the chase and for that reason had been put to death by her . . ."

Legends of the Titans rebelling against the gods are common to almost all peoples of the world. It is once again Gaster who summarizes the Hittite legend, in which a minister of the celestial beings, Kumarbi, driven from his throne which he, in his turn, had usurped, called on "the lord of the sea," who agreed to help him.

"Go to the mountain," he was told, "stretch out before it and ask it to bear a child. Within a few months the mountain will give birth to a creature made of stone. As soon as it has seen the light, take it into the abysses in the depths of the sea and place it on the shoulders of Upelluri, the giant who lives there and supports the weight of the Earth and the Sky. Day by day the stone creature will grow in height until its head strikes against the floor of the heavens; then all the gods will be tumbled from their thrones and will fly in terror."

The prophecy came true. Thus was born Ullikummi, the stone Titan against whom every defence of the gods was in vain, until Ea, the "lord of wisdom and knowledge" had a flash of genius which resolved the problem. He suggested that they should have recourse to the magic knife which at one time served to "separate the Earth from the Sky" and, in fact, this weapon destroyed the tremendous Ullikummi.

The revolt against the gods by the Titans may be interpreted, in all probability, as an outrage against the natural order of things; such an interpretation must presume in the eyes of mankind the appearance on Earth of monstrous beings. And the fact that recourse was made to the knife able to "separate the Earth from the Sky" seems to refer as much to the Creation as to a fresh divine intervention to restore the world to normality. The Titans, that is, disappear, the chaos which followed the cataclysms

Fig. 119. Must we also include among our more distant ancestors beings of this type, whose features are reproduced here on the mask of the Alaskan shamans?

vanishes and man once again takes his rightful place upon the Earth.

Belief in a being who rules Earth and Sky is widely diffused over almost the entire globe. The best-known example is certainly that of Atlas in Greek mythology who, according to Homer, lived in the heart of the Ocean and supported not only the heavens but also the earth. In an analogous way the Indians of the Chibcha

Fig. 120. Helmets and spacesuits in prehistory? The intriguing question is again posed by the so-called "Martian period" of the Tassili.

tribe in Colombia believe that the world rests on the shoulders of a giant called Chibchachum, whereas the Tlingit and various Athabascan tribes believe that the world is held in place by Hayicanako, *the Old Woman who lives beneath us.*

That creatures of stone can be conceived is an old theme of popular tradition which recurs in most parts of the world. Popular tales based on this theme are found in the northern Caucasus; and the Arab tribe of Beni Sahr in the country of Moab, literally interpreting its own name (*Sahr* means rock), call themselves descendants of a rock.

The Paressi Indians of the Mato Grosso also believe that
the first man, Darukavaitere, was made of stone and was
born of a mother, Maiso, who was also of stone.

In classical literature the myth of Deucalion and Pyrrha
is well known. It tells how, *after a universal deluge,* the
world was repopulated from the stones which these two,
the only survivors, threw behind them over their shoulders;
and almost the same story is found among the Macusi of
Guyana. An interesting trace of this belief can be discerned in the famous passage in the Odyssey (XIX, 163)
in which Penelope says to Ulysses: "Tell me of thine own
stock whence thou art, for thou are not sprang of oak or
rock, whereof old tales tell." And another echo of it can
be found in the words of the Prophet Jeremiah (2, 27):
"So is the house of Israel ashamed . . . saying to a stock:

Thou art my father; and to a *stone:* Thou hast brought me forth."

According to the Frenchman Denis Saurat, megalithic constructions, amongst them the famous dolmens, were first the work of the giants and then copied by men who were struck by their appearance and force. "Later on, in Egypt and many other places, once the giants had disappeared, men strained their feeble powers in trying to resuscitate the gods and the golden age. We have found recently in the islands round New Guinea unfortunate savages who still put up gigantic statues, dolmens and menhirs, without knowing why, just as our own ancestors no doubt did . . .

"How else can one explain the extraordinary resemblances which occur all over the earth's surface? The cromlechs in Malekula and in Brittany and in Great Britain? The giants on Easter Island? The resemblances between the legends of Greece and of Mexico?" [48]

Among those geographically closer to us but not yet mentioned are the titanic slabs of Villarfocchiardo (Valle di Susa), tracked down by Mario Salomone not far from the strange "great mask" (of which we have already spoken) of the Val Gravio, also in Piedmont (note also the presumed nuraghic remains illustrated in *Not of This World*), as well as those French ones at Saint-Benoît-du-Sault in the department of Indre, which are among the most interesting in Europe.

In Malta some of the monoliths (those reproduced here were photographed by Mr. and Mrs. Schenone, both ardent archaeologists) appear to have at one time pictured Titans. One of them shows clearly the line of the arms, the other stands high upon a heavy rock base, slender and fascinating. It has been called by a scholar "the faceless Christ."

Near the menhir are rocks which, although disfigured by weather, still bear traces of what seem to be the heads of winged beings. [49] We can say too of the famous Roc de l'Oie (Goose Rock), which weighs hundreds of tons and

Fig. 121

Fig. 122
Fig. 123
Fig. 124

Fig. 125

Fig. 126
Fig. 127

Fig. 128

170

Fig. 121. Titanic monuments have been scattered over the entire world from time immemorial; here is a dolmen known as "the giants' table." It was discovered by Mario Salomone at Villarfocchiardo in Piedmont.

Fig. 122. Another Piedmontese dolmen; it is in Val Gravio, where some mysterious graffiti are also to be seen.

Fig. 123. Also in Val Gravio we find these remains, presumably of a building of nuraghic type.

dominates the plain of Sidobre near Albi in southern France, that it was certainly erected by man.

"The largest of the menhirs and dolmens," writes Jullian, "reveal marvels of mechanics. Even if the majority of the blocks were quarried on the spot, it would still be necessary to cut them, carry them, lift them and fix them. Some of them weigh two hundred and fifty thousand kilograms (113,636 lbs.), others even more; and several

Fig. 124. Two colossal dolmens at Saint-Genoît-de-Sault (Indre, France).

have been transported over considerable distances; in the case of the megaliths at Stonehenge more than two hundred and fifty kilometers (80 mi.)." [50]

We cannot really imagine how they were transported. If we are to believe the fables current in Val Sangonetto (Piedmont), we shall be led to think of ropes. It would be reasonable to think so from the marks, especially the long, *Fig. 129* slightly oblique, horizontal fissure on the so-called "Samson's Rock." But, as Mario Salomone, who is now studying them, observes, if this had been a question of ropes, they would have had to be made of steel to leave such a track!

Not even in the remains of the "giants' houses" at *Fig. 130* Algajola (northwestern Corsica), photographed by Lamberto Camerini, can we find anything which might throw any light on the system adopted for stone-cutting or construction. The great blocks show only that they have been cut in an exceptionally regular manner, which obviously makes us think that the builders had adequate tools.

The Ghana cosmonauts

"They were of great stature, irreconcilable enemies of the gods . . . born of chaos, they loved chaos and hated the cosmos, that is to say the order and harmony established by nature," thus Nicola Turchi describes the character of the Phoenician giants, not very different, as we have seen, from that of their Hittite and Hellenic predecessors, struck, by the thunderbolts of Zeus for their impiety.

The Titan Vukub-Cakix and his family, which the *Popol Vuh* tells us massed against the gods Hun-Ahpu and Xbalanque, must have been filled with a similar spirit of contention; perhaps too the Greek sophist and writer Claudius Aelianus (175–235 A.D.), who in his *Storia Varia* tells a strange story, knew something about this; "Silenus told Midas that Europe, Asia and Africa are islands surrounded by the Ocean and beyond there is a continent,

Fig. 125. One of the famous Maltese statues which bring to mind the legendary giants. The photo, taken by Schenone, shows traces of the arms.

infinite in size, and in it live civilized beings together with others who are very tall, of a stature double ours and who live for a long time, almost double the span of years conceded to us."

"Beyond the Ocean": certainly this is not the first time that we have heard hints of "the new world" at a time when its existence must have been totally unknown in the Mediterranean area.

Here, however, it is the Titans that interest us and it seems that the American ones were not more conciliatory to their gods than the European ones. Concerning the moods and inclinations of the Titans of Sardinia, we have not much information; we have, however, the stimulating collection of photos by Professor Giovanni Lilliu [51] of the "tombs of the giants" at Bórore, Bornorva, Quartuccia and Paulilàtino.

Fig. 131

Fig. 132

In Japan the impressive creatures did not, perhaps, concern themselves much with monumental dwelling places for eternity, but they did not overlook certain delicacies.

Fig. 126. The so-called "faceless Christ" in Malta.

176

Fig. 127. Other impressive Maltese monuments photographed by the Schenones. Though disfigured by weather, some seem to have features like birds.

177

Fig. 128. Two views of the "Goose Rock," the titanic representation of a bird, which rises out of the Sidobre plain in France. Without any doubt it was placed in its present position by man.

"The huge piles of shells which are so often found in the vicinity of what are today recognized as ancient *jomon* inhabited centers are a proof of the respect in which they were held," observes William Watson of the British Museum. "In the *Hitachi-Fudo-ki*, these piles of shells have been accurately defined as middens and interpreted as traces of giants with a stride of about two meters (6.6 ft.) long." [52]

Fig. 133

Remarkably, little is known of the customs of the legendary Sao of Africa, to whom have been attributed the marvellous bronze objects discovered near Lake Chad. Two astounding terra cottas are preserved at the Musée de L'Homme in Paris; one has the "spacial" traits common to so many works of ancient and distant civilizations, the other represents an individual with a tapered head, jutting ears and mouth, which experts agree is different from any other find.

"The legends of the present-day Kotoko," Roger May writes on the subject, "say that at one time there lived in the Chad region black giants with smooth hair, from whom the Koto consider themselves to be descended. According to Arab tradition, the Titans would be white.

"Statements of this sort are confirmed by the discovery to the north of N'Guigmi of a skeleton more than 2.40 meters (8 ft.) tall. And near Goulfei there are enormous piles of very large stone blocks. The Kotoko say that it was the Sao who transported them there and speak of 'men so tall that they could look over the trees.' The archaeologist De Pedrals thinks that they were the remains of an invading white race which settled on the shores of Lake Chad and the banks of the Nile and the Niger, which became progressively assimilated with the black peoples." [53]

Another French scholar, Bonnel de Mézièreses, who is studying the fabulous empire of Ghana which in the times of the Pharoahs stretched over central and central-western Africa, discovered in the vicinity of Chad the ruins of a fortified city with five powerful circles of walls and,

Fig. 129. The so-called "Samson's Rock" at Val Sango-netto in Piedmont discovered by Salomone. According to popular legends it was dragged here by a very strong rope. The long, regular horizontal fissure at the bottom could have been made by the rope.

Fig. 130. These titanic squared stones found north of Algajola in northwestern Corsica must surely have been intended to form part of some megalithic building.

Fig. 131. A very interesting collection of photos by Professor Giovanni Lilliu of some enigmatic Sardinian buildings. (Upper left) Bórore, "Imbèrtighe," a stele with a small opening to a giant's tomb of the same name. (Upper right and lower left) Bórore, "Santu Bainzu," a general view and doorway of the stele of the giant's tomb of the same name. (Lower right) Bonorva, "Su Barattèddu," notched cornice of the giant's tomb of the same name.

Fig. 132. Another collection of photos by Professor Lilliu. (Above) Quartuccia, "Is Concas," curved frontage of a giant's tomb. (Below) Paulilàtino, "Perdu Pes"; sacred stones, known locally as betili, near one of the giants' tombs.

Fig. 133. Two strange terracotta heads of the mysterious African Sao preserved in the Musée de l'Homme at Paris; one recalls the famous "spacemen" (here too the mouth is missing and the head seems covered by a helmet), the other a humanoid type which is totally unknown.

within it, the skeleton of a man of a stature considerably greater than anything we should today regard as normal.

At this period the Titans must have already begun to decline, preserving, however, cosmic records transmitted to their direct or indirect heirs up to our own days, fantastic records of which we find traces in the present Re-

Fig. 134. (Above) The famous "gold-weight" of Ghana, used from time immemorial. Here is a very beautiful stylization of the Sun.

Fig. 135. (Below) Alongside the classical swastika are shown, in the same gold-weights, complex recurring swastikas found in many other civilizations.

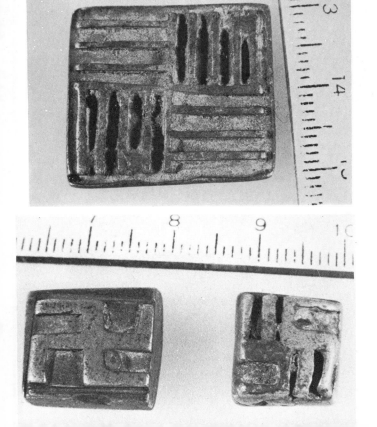

Fig. 136. Another gold-weight with the eternal spiral.

Fig. 137. A really unexpected discovery; the step-pyramid portrayed in Ghana.

186

Fig. 138. The greatest surprise of all; a strange being very similar to the Etruscan "spacemen," those of the Australians and the "Martians" of the Tassili. All the photos of the "gold-weights" have been courteously provided by Professor Paolo Durio, the well-known Turin researcher.

Fig. 139. (Following page) The most famous rock painting of the Tassili. We reproduce it here, together with the picture that follows it, to make a direct comparison easier.

187

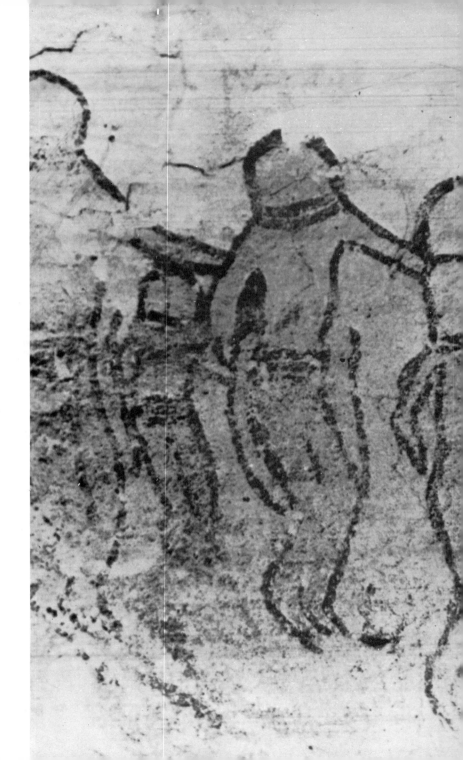

Fig. 140. The "Etruscan astronaut," to be seen in the Assisi museum.

public of Ghana, without however succeeding in tracing their origins.

The natives, questioned about the meaning of the figurines which were used as weights for gold-dust, shake their heads and smile, knowing nothing.

Fig. 134 Let us examine some of these "gold-weights," photos of which have been courteously provided by Professor *Fig. 135* Paolo Durio of the University of Turin. As well as the Sun and simple and compound swastikas symbolizing it, *Fig. 136* we also find the galaxy spiral.

Notice too the step-pyramid, which rose over the *Fig. 137* Egyptian civilization, even more majestic and dominating than those of pre-Columbian America.

There are so many surprises that they take our breath away. Here is another, which is almost incredible; the out-*Fig. 138* line of the head of an unidentifiable being, but which is *Fig. 139* in every way similar to those of the "Martians of Tassili," of the Australian "spacemen" and of the mysterious *Fig. 140* "Etruscan astronaut" in the Assisi Museum!

VI

The Weapons of Medusa

Certainly no one could say that Perseus had an easy life since the day when Acrisius, King of Argos, frightened by a prophecy, ordered him to be shut up in a chest together with his mother and thrown into the sea. He was obviously hoping that this would be one of the many successful crimes of which mythology is full. Mythology, however, is also full of many misadventures. The nefarious intention of the ruler was to turn out badly, for the chest was washed ashore on the beaches of Seriphos, one of the Cyclades.

Polydectes, king of the little island, found the girl-mother so attractive that he fell in love with her and finally decided to make her his wife. But Perseus, now grown, was not in favor of this, above all because immediately after the fortunate landing the monarch had made his mother a slave for opposing his wishes.

To forestall a future, possible *coup d'état*, Polydectes devised a perfidious plan, demanding of his future adoptive son, as a wedding gift, the head of Medusa, one of the Gorgons, even more terrible than her sisters, Sthenno and Euryale.   *Fig. 141*

Driven by pride and by that typical irresponsibility of youth still deprecated today, the young man accepted without a second thought, knowing perhaps that he was to undertake a crazy adventure. Relying on the evidence

Fig. 141. The Etruscan Gorgon's heads.

of the poets yet to come (from Simonides to Hesiod and Pindar), the three Gorgons "had tresses which were a tangle of serpents, fatal to mortals" and "their glance took from men the breath of life." How? With a simple disdainful glance, which turned to stone any who dared to look at them, or so the myths tell us.

"Poor Perseus!" We would have been tempted to say yesterday, after reference to the records of the pedants. But today, thinking of esobiology, necessarily seasoned with a little fantasy, should we not say perhaps: "Poor Gorgon!"

Expedition from Sirius

The cosmonaut, struggling in a whirlwind of mire and sludge, raised his eyes to the enormous missile which seemed to be battling against the dark sky. Perhaps it really was swaying.

"We shouldn't have landed," he thought, looking at the cylindrical capsule which was bouncing away at the end of the twisted metallic arm, "we should have let it roll away in this inferno." Nonetheless, he and his companions could not have run the risk of another landing.

Everything had seemed to go well up to the final phase of the operation; the missile, specially built to withstand the most adverse atmospheric conditions, had reached earth. The articulated arm with the sterile capsule, which was to collect, for suitable analysis, a certain quantity of the viscous mush spread over the entire planet, had emerged from the lower part of the missile.

Then some cables had snapped and a bascule had bent and broken like a tree in a hurricane. The cosmonaut had descended into this turmoil to try to repair the capsule.

He managed to breast the tempest and reach the capsule to free it from the last cable only an instant before the metal covering broke. He was dragged back on board and while he undressed the biologists busied themselves with the capsule.

"An intemperate planet," he said. "Another cataclysm . . . it must have been terrible. I saw a couple of creatures trying to get away, down there, in the caves. Poor devils! Who knows if they will survive . . ."

"In your place," commented the chief of the research section, "I should be feeling sorry for myself. What joy is there in staying here on this damned globe trying to register its convulsions?"

"They'll come to take us off!"

"Bah, don't count too much on that," the other replied. "A planet of this sort would discourage anyone from landing here."

"Wait and see."

"Till when?"

"The creatures of this planet have a much shorter lifespan than we have."

"Sure, but granted that they recover from this disaster. . . ."

Exhausted and with no more will to talk, the explorer made a gesture of indifference. He unlaced his spacesuit, wriggled out of his protective undersuit and rapidly unhitched his eight tentacles. The long antennae which sprouted from his forehead quivered in satisfaction.

He murmured, nodding towards the caves in which the creatures had taken refuge, something which in our language would mean "monsters."

We talk glibly about galactic brotherhood, of opposition to racialism on a cosmic scale"; but however well disposed we may be, we shall always feel a certain revulsion when faced with a creature which, however intelligent it may be, has an appearance different from our own. Much time will be needed and much good will before each will cease to regard the other as a "monster."

It is not hard, therefore, to imagine how bitter the fate of a group of astronauts would be like those in our tale. Isolated on Earth, they would be forced to defend themselves, and their adversaries because of their superior

Fig. 142. The very famous Gorgon of Syracuse; there is an almost identical head at Chavin de Huántar, seat of an enigmatic Peruvian culture, now extinct.

number would have ended by getting the better of their deadly and powerful weapons.

Many many legends seem to be trying to say just this to us, though couched in mythological terms, or to conceal from us the furious battles between beings very different from one another which took place upon our Earth.

We have already quoted the views of the Soviet scientist

Efremov. But we must not forget that a Greek writer who lived between about 340 and 260 B.C. founded his school on very similar views. He was Euhemerus, according to whom "the heroes and mythical personages are none other than men deified by the admiration of the peoples . . . all mythology is a transposition of historical events and the names of gods represent peoples, with their disputes and their unions . . ."

Several traditions, not only those of the Greek and Latin world, refer to the Gorgons. Gilgamesh, the Sumerian hero, fought with the monster Humbaba, who had a single eye and was able to turn whomever he looked at into stone. Humbaba, moreover, writes Gaster, "wears seven changes of raiment; he belongs therefore to the same band as the Lybian Gorgon Katovlepas, the Irish Balor, the Welsh Ispaddaden Pennkawr and the Serb Vy, all of which are monstrous orcs which repel their enemies by their lethal glances."

Let us refer once again to *Timeless Earth:* ". . . the Gorgon, whose hair, as in ancient Greece, consists of writhing serpents; but this figure was in fact known throughout antiquity, from the Etruscans to the Siculi, in Japan, China, Siam and Java, in Borneo, Hawaii and New Zealand."

We find the Gorgon again at Chavín de Huántar, the seat of an enigmatic but now extinct Peruvian culture. Here it has the features of a jaguar, but Honoré writes: "In detail it is so extremely like the Gorgon of Syracuse that one can scarcely help believing in a connection between the two: hair, nose and mouth are almost exact copies." [54]

Fig. 142

The jaguar features bring us back to another mysterious "stellar civilization"; but the very famous Syracusan Gorgon is also fanged and its serpent-locks are stylized in spirals (once again the omnipresent spiral!) as well as the volutes of the wings. Everywhere there is a hint of the cosmos, of flight. We see it even in the solar symbol and

Fig. 143. The solar sign and the symbol of flight accompany this Medusa's head from the Hypogeum of the Volumni (Perugia).

in the eagle perched on another well-known head of Medusa, the Etruscan one from the Hypogeum of the Volumni in the vicinity of Perugia.

Fig. 143

Honoré, together with several other scholars, also hints at the portrayal of the Gorgon as an octopus. It is a far from illogical hypothesis. The cephalopods, in fact, lend themselves very well to the representation of beings similar to the mythical Medusas, and the legends which have always surrounded them could have given ancient peoples further reasons for identifying them.

Fig. 144

Let us look at the figure which ornaments a famous Greek rhyton (*rhytons were recipients for libations, in the form of a bull's horn, a tapered cone or an animal's head*). It brings us back directly to the polyp on another famous find, the so-called "goblet of Ialysos" from Rhodes in suggestive red-brown coloring.

Fig. 145

Fig. 144. In all probability Medusa was often symbolized as an octopus; here we see her on a Greek rhyton.

Fig. 146

An octopus, which we could regard as closely allied to the one painted on the "Palaikastro flask" (Crete) dated about 1500 B.C., gazes at us from the fragment of a plate from Paestum,[55] now in the national museum of Gela.

Fig. 147

It is a curious fact that the upper part of this flask is reminiscent of the many and striking resemblances to "spacemen" which readers have had the chance to see in various illustrations in this book.

Fig. 148

The cephalopod motif as developed in two golden buckles from Vetulonia (one of the twelve cities of the Etruscan confederation) is really bewildering. Where are we to find the "ancestors" of these monsters? Almost everywhere, even in the heart of Amazonia, engraved by who knows what hand, in who knows how remote a past.

Fig. 145. A famous goblet from Ialysos (Rhodes), with a polyp painted in red and brown.

Fig. 146. An octopus pictured with a marine animal on a fragment of a plate from Paestum.

Fig. *149* No native, as Willy Fassio, who photographed the graffito shown here, is, would ever think of undertaking such a task or would be capable of doing so. And in the interior of this vast area where the design was found, the octopus has been completely unknown "forever"!

Here again is the polyp, accompanied by spirals and the ubiquitous "tree of life," on a sarcophagus from Fig. *150* Pachyammos which dates back to the Minoan civilization of Crete (c. 3000–1500 B.C.); and the cephalopods are equally associated with the mythical plant, the cupola Fig. *151* construction and the birds in the Eskimo calendar. Those shown in the illustration here were drawn by an artist from motifs known in the Arctic from time immemorial.

The horns of the Minotaur

Another distortion of the Gorgon concept could be the spider motif, whether in Africa or in America. In Upper Guinea, for example, spiders have very great importance in the beliefs of the Bantu, who attribute to them a leading role in their legends of "the repeopling of the Earth" (a really strange juxtaposition!) and in propitiatory and divinatory rites.

The Pima Amerindians of Uto-Aztec speech settled in Arizona, attribute the "stabilization of the world" (it is not known exactly to what this expression refers; one might be tempted to discern a hint of the return to normality after a cosmic disaster) to an "Elder Brother," equally vaguely identified, who was aided by spiders in his arduous task, whereas for the Dakotas of the north the demiurge is Iktomi, portrayed as a spider, but also as a serpent and a bird.

Fig. 147. (Opposite page) This octopus from Palaikastro in Crete has affinities with the preceding ones. It is painted on a flask which, by its very strange appearance, recalls one of the many mysterious "spacial statues."

Fig. 148.The cephalopod motif bewilderingly developed on two golden buckles from Vetulonia.

Fig. 149. In the heart of the Amazon jungle, the Turin explorer Willy Fassio photographed an octopus carved on a rock. In these regions the octopus is entirely unknown.

Fig. 150. The octopus with spiral tentacles in juxtaposition to the "tree of life" on this sarcophagus from Pachyammos (Crete), dating back to the Minoan period (c. 3000-1500 B.C.).

Fig. 151.Octopuses, "trees of life" and birds from the Eskimo calendar. Drawn by an artist of our own times, they are copies of very ancient symbols.

These are the elements dominating the history of that archaeology which seems to hypnotize us with countless cosmic allusions. Still speaking of the spider, let us take *Fig. 152* a look at the Costa Rican ornaments on which it is shown together with spirals, and at the enormous and mysterious designs in the Nasca desert of Peru, whose execution only seems possible by the use of aerial methods.[56] Here a *Fig. 153* gigantic arachnid is stylized in a stupendous manner alongside a strange reptile 180 meters (594 ft.) long (unfortunately damaged forever by the construction of the Pan- *Fig. 154* American motorway) and a very lovely bird, whose beak alone measures 100 meters (330 ft.).

Octopuses, spiders! Did our most distant ancestors find themselves face to face with beings more or less similar to such invertebrates? Or were their tentacles, like the hissing locks of the Gorgons, in reality the organs of some quite different species, parts of their equipment, antennae?

Less traditional scholars, who are disposed to examine the "spacial hypothesis" with *a priori* skepticism, consider either one or the other theory to be possible, naturally until there is proof to the contrary.

Don't the Kappas (the mysterious Japanese "men of the canebrakes") seem, from the descriptions which have been handed down to us, to have been proboscideans? Here, too, is another piece of information: "Tschi Pen Lao, of the University of Peking, has discovered curious drawings in the mountains of Hunan and on an island in Lake Tung-ting. Made about forty-five thousand years before Christ, these granite carvings portray people with large trunks and cylindrical craft. It is difficult to admit the existence of space-helmets and spaceships so long ago, yet what other explanation can one offer?" [57]

It seems rash to support the theory of the Kappas, yet science today is unable to suggest any explanation other than that put forward by Professor Kitamura.[58] Even though reluctantly in certain circles, it must be admitted that the four slender "horns" on the protective headgear

Fig. 152. Sketches of some of the gigantic designs in the Nasca desert: birds (5, 12, 14, 15), fishes (9, 10), llamas (3), monkey (7), spider (16), reptile (18). The scale shown at the foot of each drawing by a double line in each case represents fifty meters (165 ft.).

of these bizarre creatures is very similar to antennae since they cannot possibly be bony excrescences and the curious "ornaments" of other Japanese statuettes of the *jomon* period, statuettes which, even as those better known,

Fig. 155

Fig. 153. Nasca: the representation of a strange reptile a hundred and fifty meters (492 ft.) long has unfortunately been damaged by the construction of the Pan-American motor road.

Fig. 154. The beak alone of this bird stylized in so evocative a manner is a hundred meters (330 ft) long. It is only visible from an airplane as are the other Nasca figures; was the supervision of these very ancient designs, therefore, carried out from above?

Fig. 155. Three Ainu statuettes. The first is from the middle jomon *period (note the feline expression which, with the claws, recalls the mysterious Kappas); the other two belong to the late* jomon *period and should be regarded as further versions of the famous Japanese "spacial* dogu."

called *dogu*, from whose designs working spacesuits have been made,[59] seem equally to represent beings from outer space.

The horn symbol seems everywhere to have astral significance, from the prehistoric Sahara to Zimbabwe, from Persia to India, from America to northern and central Europe and to the Mediterranean world.

In Mesopotamia these horns sometimes represent the Moon and sometimes Venus. The Babylonians knew the "horns of Venus" according to R. N. C. Bowen. They describe the crescent of the planet and its phases, similar to those of the moon. But the "horns of Venus" are invisible to the naked eye. How then could the priests of ancient Babylonia observe them without telescopes? [60]

Fig. 156
There is a warrior with a horned helmet on the Mesopotamian stelle of Tello-Lagash known as the "stele of the vultures" and his image is dominated by two stars which shine above a curious conical formation; nor is the "tree of life" lacking; it is a little lower down.

Fig. 157
King Hor of the Egyptian XIII dynasty is pictured with a bizarre pair of horns terminating in two raised hands. The view of those who see in this a symbol of antennae (of instruments, that are able to "receive," to "be aware," even as are hands) is hazardous; yet it is difficult to exclude it, even by assuming that they are stylizations of animal organs of touch and scent, from which antennae have taken their name.

Fig. 158
We see again in Crete the horns which, in relief, decorate the walls of the Sardinian "Grotto of the Elephant." This is nothing exceptional since we must remember that the island of Crete is the homeland of the fabulous Minotaur, but we find on the island even more evocative allusions to the fascinating mysteries of the past.

Fig. 159
Some small plaques of beaten gold seem to outline squared "spacial " faces with four protuberances on the top and two birds at the sides. There have been many hypotheses about these; there has been talk of the reproduction of temples dedicated to marine deities, to whom appeals would be made before setting out on voyages, and the birds have induced others to speak openly of one of the many "Noah's arks," which the whole world knows, but not one of the explanations suggested is fully satisfactory.

Fig. 160
One thing is clear; the so-called "horned crown" of the plaques has its equivalent in those of the clay idols found at Gazi near Herakleion, in the immediate vicinity of Knossos, where rose the kingdom of the legendary Minos, unfortunate father of the Minotaur.

Fig. 161
The idols in question, with head and arms raised at right angles forming a trident,[61] are closely associated with the three "horns" of a mask discovered near the gateway of Knossos itself.

Fig. 156. The Mesopotamian "stele of the vultures"; once
again the association of horns, the "tree of life" and
astral symbols is remarkable.

The fact that the trident had in ancient times an almost
worldwide diffusion is Sybilline. We come across it as
much in Italy and France as in European and Asiatic
Russia, as much in Africa as in America, and not only as
a tool or a weapon. Figured as three-pronged lightning,
we find it gripped by Asiatic and Mediterranean divinities.

To go back to the Cretan clay idols; it occurs to us at
once to compare them with the figure of "the bearded

Fig. 162

Fig. 163

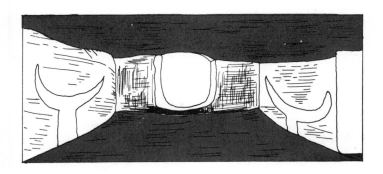

Fig. 158. Interior of the Sardinian "Grotto of the Elephant," with horns carved in relief on the walls.

Fig. 159. Many fantastic hypotheses have been suggested for these Mycenaean gold plaques with upper protuberances, birds and strange central designs.

Fig. 157. (Opposite page) The "horns terminating in two hands" of this statuette of the Egyptian ruler Hor are regarded by some scholars as symbolizations of antennae.

Fig. 160. The clay idols of Herakleion; the head and arms form a trident.

god" from Tiahuanaco, which some scholars identify as Poseidon, considering him a legendary king of Atlantis.[62] It must not be forgotten that Minos asked from Poseidon, according to the legend, the dispatch of a bull in order to confirm his own right to the throne; hence the sequence of events which led to the birth of the Minotaur.

Hercules and the flying saucer

As is known, the merit of destroying the Cretan monster belongs to Theseus. But this hero [63] was the protagonist of many other exploits; he conquered giants and frighten-

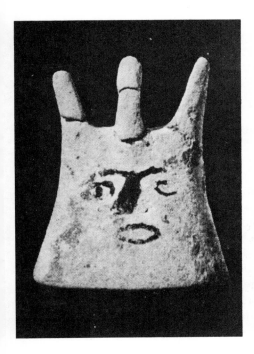

Fig. 161. This very
strange tricorn mask
was discovered a
short distance from
Herakleion, near the
Knossos gate (resi-
dence of the legen-
dary Minos, king of
Crete).

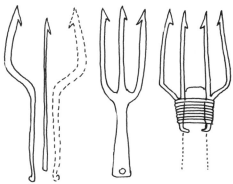

Fig. 162. Three types of prehistoric trident; from left to
right those of Peschiera del Garda, of La Tène and of
Lake Peipsi (Esthonia, Soviet Union).

Fig. 164

Fig. 165

ing animals. He supported Hercules in his expedition against the Amazons and aided his friend Pirithous, Prince of the Lapiths, in his war against the centaurs. What sort of creatures were they? Did they have a human torso and a horse's body, as we are accustomed to imagine them? No, such representations were unknown in Homer's time. He speaks of them as violent beings "with bristling locks."

The ancient Hellenic legends find strange correlation with Guatemalan traditions. The centaurs of Thessaly called themselves "sons of the mist," as the savage outriders of the American skies called themselves "born of the clouds and the Sun," and these last, like their Greek fellows, seem to have cultivated the bad habit of seizing other people's wives. Two further details, however, make us think even more deeply: the Guatemalan representation of the "solar beings" which recalls that of the Gorgons, and the battle fought against them by a hero whose name varies from people to people (no wonder, since the record links us to pictures from ancient epochs incapable of interpretation) but whose exploits are similar, in certain particulars, to those of Perseus, son of Danäe and Zeus, who impregnated the girl in the form of a shower of gold.[64]

Let us examine a little more closely the adventures of Perseus charged, as we have said, with gaining possession of the head of Medusa. A mission doubtlessly hazardous and which would have been suicidal if its protagonist had not been able to count on the aid of Hermes and Athena. The former counselled him to provide himself with suitable weapons from the northern nymphs (whose dwelling place was known only to the Graiae, huge birds with human heads), who gave him a sword to match the shield

Fig. 163. (Opposite page) Teshup, Hittite god of the storm, grips the three-pronged lightning.

given him by Athena and flew with him to the land of the Gorgons "in the extreme west . . . where were the Hesperides and Atlantis."

The Hellenic legend is a real science-fiction story, and is revealed as such by the allusion to the petrifying gaze of the three sisters. Could it be a question of some unknown weapon? Let us say openly that it was, since before marrying Andromeda Perseus had to contend with a rival for the maiden's hand, Phineus, whose army he decimated, hurling against his enemies the rays that sprang from the severed head of Medusa.

The "rod which causes sleep" and the winged shoes of Hermes, which Perseus received in the land of the Hyperboreans (which was perhaps not dissimilar to that of the Graiae [65]), might well be the equivalents of a poison-gas pistol and an exceedingly fast form of aerial transport. He

Fig. 164. The "centaur of Vulci," an Etruscan sculpture of about 600 B.C.

216

was also given a satchel which had the property of taking the form of whatever it contained and a helmet rendering invisible whoever wore it.

The "winged feet" recur in some legends of Central and South America, where we often see them pictured on vessels used for ritual purposes, and the less conventional weapons frequently make their appearance in pre-Columbian designs.

"Good God! It looks like a tommy-gun!" an archaeologist friend exclaimed, alluding to one of the implements grasped by Quetzalcoatl in a reproduction in the Borgia Codex which pictures him armed with exceedingly strange equipment opposing personages equipped with weapons which bode no good (look at the small central figure).

Let us continue the jest; in a similar way we can compare with *panzerfausts* or bazookas the weapons with which the god Xipe Totec, venerated considerably before the arrival of the Aztecs, by the Mixtecs, the Zapotecs and the Pipil, is provided. His name means "the flayed one" and refers to the bloody ceremonies in the course of which the priests of Ancient Mexico arrayed themselves in the skins of slaughtered enemies. But could not these rites (even as the custom which still exists today when the Siberian hamans dress themselves in bearskins) refer to that "double skin" of which we have spoken earlier and which a very slight effort of the imagination might induce us to identify with a spacesuit, an overall or, at the very least, some kind of protective clothing?

As to the helmet, let us compare it, still in jest, be it understood, with a space-helmet and we shall see how easily it would make us unrecognizable. Who knows how the word "invisible" might be translated in terms of fable? We believe that it would be somewhat difficult, for example, to recognize the features of a human being behind the armor seen on the very evocative "Lunigiana steles" now in the archaeological museum at Spezia, where there can also be admired a "mouthless man" who, though in a

Fig. 166

Fig. 167

Fig. 168

Fig. 169

Fig. 170

217

Fig. 165. The Sun, similar to a Gorgon, stands out on this stele from Cozumalhuapa (Guatemala), together with other cosmic symbols and a strange "worshipper."

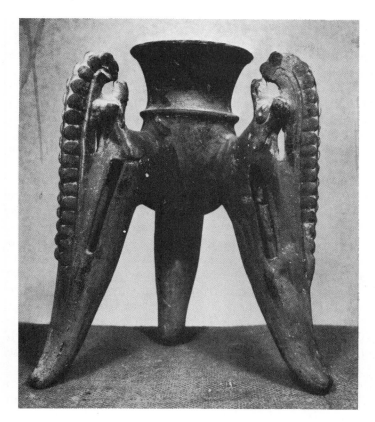

Fig. 166. The "winged feet" occur not only in Mediterranean mythology but also in several American forms; here they are represented on a polychrome tripod from the province of Limón (Costa Rica).

different way, might equally express the idea of invisibility.

Fig. 171

As far as the sword and shield of Perueus are concerned, "which enabled him to confront armored men invulnerable to every cutting edge," it seems reasonable to us to display a certain scepticism. A sword and a shield of this nature could not have existed at that time. Nor is that all; metals of any sort "could not" have been known because the legend of Perseus, like that of Hercules, is anterior to the Age of Bronze and is firmly linked with palaeolithic times!

Fig. 172

"Herakles (Hercules in Latin mythology) was not a Greek because when his myth was widespread Greece had not yet been born. A distinguished author has discovered that *herakles* was not a proper name but a word signifying, in archaic Crete, an official with duties analogous to those of the Carthaginian *suffetes*," [66] writes Charpentier.

He too regards the legends as distortions of real events. It would really be interesting to find the key to the twelve proverbial Labors to which the hero, as everyone knows, was condemned in order to expiate his crime (he had killed three of his sons in a crisis of madness provoked by Hera) and to win immortality for himself. Unfortunately, that is not possible. We must content ourselves with vague references, from which, however, as in the case of Perseus, emerge a romantic and Utopian epic.

The first Labor finds Herakles stifling in the embrace of the Lion of Nemea (a valley of the Argolid), which no weapon could wound. Was this beast related to those menacing felines with yawning jaws which we find among the bronzes of the so-called "tomb of Midas" from Gordium in south-western Anatolia, in the Etruscan necropolises and in the incense-burners of the enigmatic "Group X" (Ballana, Egypt), whose head is so similar to that of a Chinese dragon?

Fig. 173

Fig. 174

Fig. 175

Fig. 176

We find them guarding the entrances of Christian churches. Even though they recall to mind far more ancient representations, they have, nonetheless, lost their original significance. All the same, fascinating allusions lead us back across space and time. Have we not seen the feline rivalling the dragon in the Far East; have we not admired it alongside the serpent in pre-Columbian America, just as in the cathedral of S. Vigilio at Trento?

Fig. 177

Let us give free rein to our imagination and project

Fig. 167. Quetzalcoatl, equipped with bizarre accoutrements, confronts beings with devices which bode little good (from the Borgia Codex, 19).

Fig. 168. The scepters of this ancient Mexican god really do resemble strange weapons. His name is Xipe Totec, which means "the flayed one": in the "double skin," however, as in other magical vestments, some scholars see a sort of spacesuit.

Fig. 169. A "spaceman of the Lunigians," seen full-face and in profile.

upon our screen the struggle of Herakles against the proud "cat-man" from space, even as we shall see him, in the second, third and ninth Labor respectively, facing the strangest of beasts: the Hydra of Lerna, the nine-headed serpent which infested the Argolid (and there is another serpent in the saga of our hero, the one which personified the river Achelous), the unchained Erymanthean boar, the man-eating mares of Diomedes, perhaps mirrored in the beautiful Etruscan winged horses.

Fig. 178

Fig. 179

We do not know what the Ceryneian stag, with golden

Fig. 170. Another stele of the Lunigians, preserved, like the preceding one, in the archaeological museums at Spezia. Here too we are confronted by the enigmatic "beings without mouths" which, in every part of the globe, have led to the formulation of fantastic theories.

antlers and copper hooves, captured by the hero in his fourth Labor, may represent. The shadow of the Minotaur looms over the sixth, the eighth and the tenth exploit, which pledged Herakles to clean the Augean stables (which he did "simply" by diverting the course of two rivers), to tame the fearsome bull of Crete, and to capture the oxen of Geryon, a monster with three bodies, living in a "western island" called Erytheia.

223

Fig. 171. This drawing of a very strange "faceless man" is also in the Spezia archaeological museum.

On this occasion the hero created, without more ado, the Straits of Gibraltar by separating two mountains subsequently known as the "Pillars of Hercules." Everything leads us to believe that in this case (as with the diversion of the rivers and the twelfth Labor, the capture of Cerberus, when, it is said, the whole earth trembled), there are vague and distorted hints of cataclysms which changed the appearance of vast areas.

Fig. 172. Herakles, he t with the "double skin" (c tail from Vulci, near T[...] quinia).

Fig. 173. The impressive lion's head found in the "tomb of Midas" at Gordium in southwestern Anatolia.

Fig. 174. The "lion of Vulci."

225

Fig. 175. An incense-burner in the form of a lion from the enigmatic "Group X" (Ballana, Egypt). It is reminiscent of Far Eastern forms, whereas those of Figs. 173 and 174 are closer to the mythical jaguars of central and southern America.

Here as with the oxen of Geryon, we are once more in the realms of science fiction. "It is told that Herakles, outraged by the burning rays of the setting sun, shot his arrows against it," writes Ramorino, "whereupon Helios, in admiration of such audacity, *allowed him the use of his golden boat, made in the form of a goblet,* in which the hero could cross the ocean and reach Erytheia."

A prototype of a "flying saucer"? We should not be surprised seeing that in the adventures of the indefatigable Superman of antiquity not even spaceships were lacking.

Fig. 180

There is a definite hint of the pre-Aztec "night eagle" (that beautiful winged creature of perverted habits) in his struggle against the terrible Stymphalian birds, nested in Arcadia, "with talons, wings and beaks of bronze and feathers also of bronze, which they hurled like arrows."

Could these really be aerial vehicles? We can hardly conceive any different idea of these metallic flying missile throwers. And all the elements of the most ancient legend appear to be concentrated in the Hittite group of Kargamish which shows the man-eagle holding in leash two felines strangely similar to those of pre-Columbian America, dominated, however, by an enormous human figure which seems able to control the destiny of all men. *Fig. 181*

During his seventh Labor Herakles comes to grips with the Amazons, as did so many arrogant males of antiquity, and seizes the girdle of their queen, Hippolita. Could this object have been something similar to a comic-strip anti-gravity girdle?

Given the items already considered, this hypothesis should not be rejected out of hand. And it becomes even less improbable when we try to grasp the significance of the eleventh exploit. The literal meaning really cannot be regarded as satisfactory; it would be childish and futile for

Fig. 176. As in the oriental representations, though with a completely different significance, changing through the centuries, the lion is opposed in Christian symbolism to the dragon. Here is a sculpture from the northeast door of the cathedral of S. Vigilio at Trento (mid-thirteenth century).

227

Fig. 177. A lion and a serpent guard the central window
of the cathedral of S. Vigilio at Trento.

228

Fig. 178. Herakles struggling with the river Achelous, here represented as a man-serpent, on an ancient amphora.

a hero to be sent to steal apples, even if they were of gold. All the same, our hero flies to the garden of the Hesperides and profits by the occasion to strike down the giant Antaeus.

"The Latins regarded this combat as a historical fact," Charpentier tells us, "and Pliny established precisely the spot at which the tomb of Antaeus could be found: at Lixus, facing the mythical garden of the Hesperides. He gives exact measurements of the giant's tomb; it was sixty cubits long, that is to say about seventeen meters (62 ft.). The Romans believed this so firmly that when they occupied Tingitania, a general ordered excavations to be made on the summit of the Charf (an isolated *hillock near Tangiers*) to look for the famous tomb. And it is said that the legionaries discovered there a quantity of bones." [67]

It is really a strange story, this story of the giant, linked to many other myths. He was the son of Poseidon, god of the sea and the Earth; his wife owed her birth to Atlas, the Titan who supported the world. The ancient traditions have preserved the names of his other daughters, three of

Fig. 179. These very beautiful Etruscan chargers "in the service of the gods" (shown here in a detail from a temple at Tarquinia) are perhaps reminiscent of the horses of Diomedes mastered by Herakles.

Fig. 180. A splendid Mexican ornament in the form of an eagle's head decorated with spirals; it recalls perhaps the pre-Aztec "celestial bird" which, like the birds mastered by Herakles, launched its own feathers as projectiles.

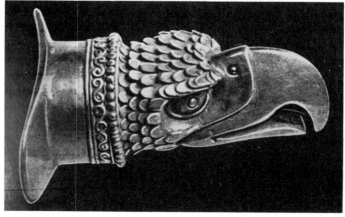

Fig. 181. (Opposite page) Two felines, remarkably similar to those of pre-Columbian America, are held in leash by a being with an eagle's head in a Hittite group of basalt from Kargamish.

which give us reason to think: Aegle, the white; Hespere, the black; and Erytheia; the red, who must have stood as godparent to the "western isle," a place beyond the ocean, as is explicitly stated.

There is nothing strange in the fact that in or about present-day Tangiers both white and black races should be known. But that in prehistoric times a red race settled much farther to the west beyond the sea should have been known is really astonishing.

What other reasonable deduction can we draw, however, from legends which agree so perfectly in certain details?

VII

Firebirds

"After the death of Hyperion, the myths say, his kingdom was divided among the sons of Uranus, the most
famous of whom were Atlas and Chronos. Atlas received
as his share the coastal regions of the ocean and not only
gave the name of Atlantids to their people, but also gave
the name of Atlas to the highest mountain of the country."

So wrote the Greek Diodorus Siculus (who lived at the
time of Julius Caesar) in his monumental *Biblioteka*. He
was certainly not the sort of person who believed blindly
in the religion of his times, since he added a very rational
explanation of a well-known story.

"It is also told that Atlas brought to perfection the
science of astronomy and that he was the first to teach its
doctrines to the human race; *for that reason the idea is
held that the whole sky is supported on his shoulders*."

If we accept that Hyperion, one of the Titans, son of
Uranus and Mother Earth (Gea), was regarded as "father
of the Sun, the Moon and the Dawn" as symbolic, we shall
also have to consider the beliefs to which Diodorus Siculus
refers in the following passage as symbolic:

"Atlas, the myth goes on, had seven daughters, called as
a group the Atlantides; their personal names were, however, Maia, Electra, Taygete, Sterope, Merope, Alcyone
and Celaeno. They mated with the gods and the most famous of the heroes and their descendants were the first
ancestors of the greater part of the human race. . . After

their deaths the daughters of Atlas were enthroned in the skies and given the name of the Pleiades. . ."

Whoever has read *Not of This World* and remembers the references of so many peoples to the Pleiades will find these coincidences somewhat strange. It is not always a question of pretty girls pouring down upon the earth; it is to this constellation that so many stories refer to persons who come from the skies to lend a hand to men and help them to achieve considerable advances in civilization.

It was from the Pleiades therefore, according to some scholars who think that they have correctly interpreted the most ancient traditions of Asia and America, that the "Great Brothers" came, who brought to the highest level of development, lands now swallowed by the sands or submerged by the waters, among the most famous of them, Mu and Atlantis.

Expedition from the Pleiades

"This is a fine mess," said the taller of the astronauts, looking around. "This crash will pin man to prehistory for hundreds of thousands of years."

The shorter astronaut adjusted his respirator. His colleague, who had come from a different planet, had no need of one. "It will mean the end of all these strange creatures," he observed, pointing at the bizarre figures which thronged the edges of the path from the spaceship to the caves.

"They were already doomed to extinction," his companion retorted.

They had touched down on Earth after one of the great cataclysms which from time to time overwhelmed that planet. They had landed on a high plateau surrounded by mountain torrents, and had found safety there as had members of the last races surviving the ascent of the superior being and the birth pangs of the globe.

A Neanderthal stretched out his long arm towards the topboots of the cosmonauts and muttered something unin-

*. 182. (Above) The humanoid jaguar from La Venta abasco) with "stellar fringes" symbolizing flight. (Be-) the "beast of Teotihuacán," it too Mexican.

telligible. A little farther away a hairy giant showed his teeth; he swung a huge branch, brandishing it like a club. Some hominids, small and agile as monkeys, chittered inimically among the shattered trees.

There was a gleam of pity in the glance of one of the space explorers, the one with the flat face with sunken eye-sockets. In the large eyes of his companion nothing could be discerned.

Those eyes were like a cat's; and like a cat's, they narrowed to slits as his mouth opened over pointed teeth in a hideous grin.

It was not a grin but a smile and the creature towards which the two advanced knew it. It rose from the entrance to the cave, setting aside the spear on which it had been working, and smiled in its turn.

The being with the cat face pointed at the fur clad creature: "This is the master of the planet," he said. Then he added something which, were it said today, would sound like *Homo Sapiens*.

Were these cat-faced astronauts, who landed on Earth and were deified by the first inhabitants of the globe, pledged to assist them, as colonists or as shipwrecked space mariners, in their ascent?

This account of our third Utopian fable might conceal a valid hypothesis, taking the place of the confused records and bewildering images of the cat-men which are to be found throughout all Central and South America.

Some very strange stylizations (other than those illustrated in previous books) have come to light in the "new world." Here, for instance, is the humanoid jaguar of the "La Venta culture" (Tabasco) with the typical "solar fringes" indicating flight on what seems a head-covering; and here too are similar fringes on the outstretched claws of the "Toetihuacan beast," it too Mexican.

Feline figures (see the third from the left) look at us also from the ancient Mediterranean world, together with others from northern Europe which are unidentifiable; of

Fig. 182

Fig. 183

Fig. 183. (From the left) The "spacemen" of the Cyclades (3000 B.C.), of Tell Ashmar in Mesopotamia (c. 2300-1900 B.C.), of Troy (c. 2500-2300 B.C.) and again of Tell Ashmar (3000 B.C.).

the three amber idols from Chernyakhovsk (East Prussia, Fig. 184
Soviet Union) the central one illustrated strongly recalls
the statuettes of the archiac period in Ecuador, while the
one on the right seems to be wearing a clumsy spacesuit

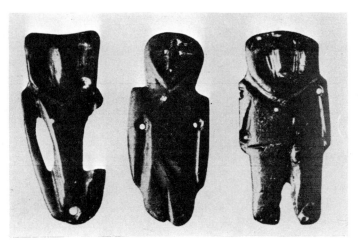

Fig. 184. Three idols in amber from Chernyakhovsk (East Prussia, Soviet Union), dating back to 2000 B.C..

similar to those invented for our own explorers at the beginning of the "astronautic era."

Fig. 185 The mysterious Peruvian Nasca civilization provides us, among many other things, with a ceramic in which are synthetized all the elements which are typical of the ancient American cultures, from the jaguar-like features to those of the serpent, with a head-covering showing two eyes and a mouth; is it a mask intended to be drawn over the face or, as the supporters of the "cosmic theory" would assert, the ingenuous reproduction of a space-helmet?

The hypothesis doubtless appears significant if we compare this ceramic with other statuettes, above all one from Fig. 186 Paracas (central Peru), a terra-cotta figurine without a face but with indications which convey to us the idea of insulating garments covering the upper part of the torso, the abdomen and the lower joints.

They differ only a little, in the concept which presumably inspired their creators, from the stone idols discovered Fig. 187 at Aviz in Spain, and at Idanha-a-Nova in Portugal. The hints of human form and the resemblances to some flying creature can be discerned in a clay idol from Vrsac, though it recalls analogous American, Asian and African syntheses; but we are left astonished and perplexed by that figurine Fig. 188 found at Klicevac (that too in Yugoslavia), which as well as solar symbols and spirals, has designs, the "Pectoral arrows," for example, which only have equivalents among pre-Columbian civilizations.

There are also figures, like that on a bizarre vase from Fig. 189 Anatolia, which recall the American "flat-headed men." Here are far more detailed portrayals of these in other Fig. 190 regions; humanoid and spacesuit seem to be mirrored on a vessel, unique in the world, from the Valle del Cauca in Columbia; and who could really say what is grasped in the Fig. 191 hands of the stone being on a Toltec stele, with its curious "helmet" and a large spacesuit valve? Or is it some unknown weapon?

238

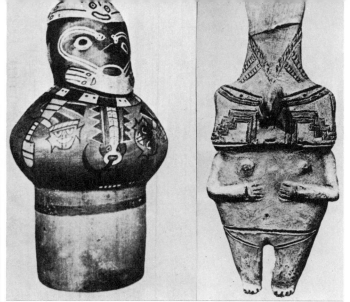

Fig. 185. (Left) A Nasca "spacial" ceramic (Peru), in which seem to be mingled all the most enigmatic elements of the ancient American cultures.

Fig. 186. (Right) The faceless figurine from Paracas (central Peru) suggests insulating garments, at least for the upper part of the torso, the abdomen and the lower limbs.

Fig. 187. Compare these two stone idols with the figures above; that on the left was found at Aviz in Spain, the other at Idanha-a-Nova in Portugal.

Fig. 188. Vague hints of human figures or divinities can be found in a clay female figure (on the left) from Klicevac, and in the idol, also of clay, from Vrsac, both in Yugoslavia, dating from 1600-1200 B.C.

The statuettes of the "Vicus culture," about which Federico Patellani writes in the review *Atlas*, are without doubt easier for us to understand.

"Does the obscurity of the Peruvian tombs recently excavated in the north of the country near the foothills of Mt. Vicus (district of Morropon) hide the secrets of a very ancient civilization, hitherto unknown. . . ? What are the links between the Vicus civilization and that of Salinar and Galinazo, which have similar characteristics? How is one to explain the discovery of a hoard of ceramics so similar to the Vicus in the peninsula of Paracas, eleven hundred kilometers (1760 mi.) from Piura? How can one explain the links between Vicus and the regions farther north in the American continent in the composition of the ceramics and the designs of the goldsmith's work? Is it a case of convergence or of diffusion? If it is a question of diffusion, what is the direction of the influences? Is it not logical to think that in the Vicus civilization and in the influences dependent upon it one can discern a case of ebb and flow?"

"These are fascinating questions but for the moment no one is in a position to give exhaustive and definite replies. The long-delayed discovery of the Vicus civilization has overturned the dating and cataloguing of the pre-Columbian ceramics of Peru and neighboring cultures."

Fig. 192

The adherents of the "astronautical theory," faced with the features and expressions on the Vicus ceramics, have been unable to avoid the temptation of regarding them as the result of the mating of the "cat-men" with the representatives of a race existent before their supposed arrival,

Fig. 189. One might describe this vase which was found in Anatolia as typically American in detail.

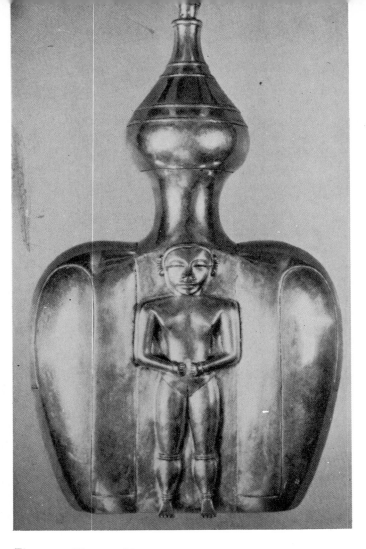

Fig. 190. Humanoid and "spacesuit" pictured in a find unique in the world, a gold and copper vessel from the Cauca Valley in Colombia.

242

Fig. 191. (Opposite page) This strange being on a Tolte stele crushes in its hands an unknown object, interprete by some as the valve of a spacesuit, by others as weapon.

Fig. 193

Fig. 194

thus, even without wishing to do so, aligning themselves with Diodorus Siculus.

That this "arrival" may have been symbolized by a bizarre bird and by the famous motif of the "spacemen without mouths" on a vase from the Vicus civilization is a problem surely destined to remain unsolved for a very long time. Today we can only sketch out some fantastic hypotheses, mainly supported by the extraordinary similarity of the Mexican "boot-tombs" (the most famous is the so-called "Osario," excavated from beneath a pyramid at Chichén-Itzá) to those discovered in the foothills of Mt. Vicus. Here we find, buried at a great depth, metal artifacts of tubular form whose use no one has been able to

Fig. 192. Statuettes representing the very ancient Peruvian people known (from the place of their discovery) as Vicus. Their resemblance to the famous "cat-men" is undeniable.

244

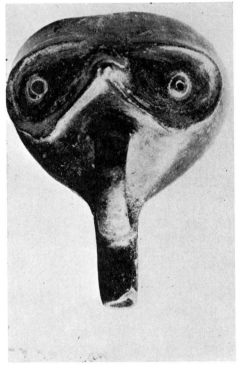

Fig. 193. A bird with outspread wings and a vase which recalls the "mouthless spacemen," both from the mysterious Vicus culture.

explain; there is reason to suppose, indeed, that these objects are far earlier in date than the culture itself and were preserved as a symbol of immortality!

It is intresting to note that objects of aluminum (a metal isolated only in 1827 and industrial production of which began only in 1886) of a very remote period, but not dateable, were found in 1956 in the Gobi desert by a Russo-Chinese expedition. We cannot even guess what purpose they served, but perhaps we may get an inkling if we regard them as a ritual imitation of the "command batons" of the shamans or of the pre-Columbian "sceptres" (see Fig. 33).

Nor is that all; similar cylindrical batons, about twenty centimeters long, whose use also remains a mystery, have been discovered in the French and Spanish caves of Arudy, Lourdes, Isturitz, Uornos de la Peña, as well as in Hungary, in western and southern Germany,[68] and in Japan, and in Australia.[69]

"Only to know one another"

Fig. 195 A spellbinding Aztec head with empty eyesockets gazes at us from Teteoinan in Mexico. Solar symbols and spirals stand out from the sides of the head. It is described simply as a "female divinity," but that is purely a definition of convenience.

It is a face which speaks to us of pain and desperation as do others which we already know and which have the unmistakable features of the "cat-men."

"At Monte Albán," writes Roberto Calcagno, "the Zapotecs set up at the foot of an imposing edifice a series of stone tablets showing figures believed to be dancers.

Fig. 196 "The series is in fact known as the *Galeria de los Danzantes* (the Dancers' Gallery). On one of the western stones is depicted a crouching man. His face has unusual features which seem distorted by suffering. His head, instead of having the usual elaborate ornaments, is covered

246

Fig. 194. On the left a Vicus "boot-tomb," on the right
an analogous tomb excavated from beneath a pyramid at
Chichén-Itzá in Yucatan.

247

Fig. 195. The nightmare "Aztec goddess" of Teteoinan.

by a close-fitting cap; nor has his body anything that re-calls the magnificence of pre-Columbian vestments. It is wrapped in a sort of overall, with little circular openings similar to the large eyelets of a spacesuit.

Fig. 197   "To the east is another 'dancer' in an attitude that clearly indicates great pain, with the face contracted in a grimace and the arms crossed over the belly. Here too we see the 'helmet' and the 'overall.'

"Similar characteristics are evident also in the other

248

Fig. 196. Suffering marks the features and the movements of this "dancer" from Monte Albán.

Fig. 198

figures, especially those in the western section, where some of the dancers have their legs stretched wide apart, with heads thrown back. The clothing does not change. "What is the real meaning of this work? It seems to us quite unsuitable to insist on the idea of 'dancers.' Such unusual features, the grimaces of pain and the nature of the clothing are really strange. Let us suppose, on the contrary, that some chance should have compelled a group of cosmonauts from another planet to make a forced landing on Earth. A tragic irony would have made their manifestations of pain later appear as a dance."

This is undoubtedly a daring hypothesis, but it is one easily compatible with the obsessional expressions which appear time and time again in the *Aztec Songs:* [70]

> *Does one really live here on Earth?*
> *Not for all time, only for a little!* (1)
> *We come only to sleep,*
> *Only to dream.*
> *It is not true, it is not true*
> *That we have come to live upon Earth!* (2)
> *But what can my heart do, if it is in vain*
> *That we come to live upon Earth,*
> *To flower in vain?* (3)
> *Where, O my heart, is the place of life?*
> *Where is my true home?*
> *Where my true dwelling place?*
> *I suffer, here upon Earth.* (4)

In some passages these hints at a place of origin which is certainly not on our planet are very clear indeed. The distinction between the place in which their ancestors were born and that where they now live (*"on Earth"*) are evident, and the allusion to the "casket" and the "ark" are curious. The contrast between the passage *descent in the center of the Sky* and that of *"in the heart of the Earth"* seems to explain on the one hand the hope of re-

Fig. 197. Once again the expression of pain in the dancers wearing helmets and close-fitting overalls pictured at Monte Albán.

Fig. 198. Another evocative representation of the so-called Mexican "space dancers."

turn to a stellar homeland and on the other the fear of
death on an inhospitable globe:

> *Here the flowery death is born.*
> *Those who took form in Tlapalla,*
> *Our ancestors, reached Earth . . .* (5)
> *What shall we sing, my friends?*
> *In what shall we rejoice?*
> *There alone our song lives,*
> *Where our ancestors were born.*
> *On Earth, where they lived . . .*
> *I suffer here on Earth . . .*
> *He who gives life conceals*
> *Men in a casket and in an ark. . . .*
> *But shall I see them? Shall my eyes see*
> *The faces of my father and my mother?*
> *Can they offer me their song,*
> *Their words, which I search for?*
> *Here there is no one,*
> *They have left us as orphans, here on Earth.* (6)

And again:

> *Where shall I go? Alas, where shall I go?*
> *Doubt hangs heavily upon me.*
> *Perhaps to the House of God,*
> *Whence one descends, in the center of the sky,*
> *Or here where one descends in the heart of the*
>   *Earth?* (7)

Two wall-paintings of the so-called *Templo de las
Caritas* at Cempoala have been interpreted as symbols of
the Sun and Moon; but it is scarcely necessary to abandon
oneself to the wings of science fiction to see in the first
(in company with some eastern and western scholars), the
quadrant of a navigational instrument and in the second,
something that makes one think of a space vehicle. And

Fig. 199

253

in the *Aztec Songs* there is no lack of references to such means of transport:

> *Green serpent of the lightning . . .* (8)
> *You are the quechól bird, color of fire,*
> *Which flies across the plain*
> *In the kingdom of death.* (9)
> *Huitzilopochtli, the warrior,*
> *He who acts and is on high*
> *Follows his own path . . .*
> *O marvellous dweller among the clouds . . .*
> *O dweller in the region of the frozen wings. . . .*
> *He causes the walls of fire to fall down*
> *Where the feathers are gathered.*
> *Thus he wages war*
> *And subdues the peoples . . .*
> *Eager for war, the Flaming One descends,*
> *He rages where the whirling dust arises.*
> *Come to our aid!*
> *There is war, there is burning.*
> *Those of Pipitlan are our enemies.* (10)

If we think of a race fallen from the stars, more or less similar to the human race and well disposed to it, the meaning of other verses becomes very clear:

> *Friends, a mission has driven us to the world . . .* (11)
> *It is true that we shall become friends,*
> *It is true that we shall live upon Earth,*
> *But the time will come when*
> *You will tire of our friendship.* (12)

The idea of this strange friendship will be confirmed, as well as others, which seem clearly to refer to the stay on Earth of beings from space. As the songs are interpreted here, as they may well have been interpreted by the Aztecs themselves, they are not to be analysed scientifically and

Fig. 199. These designs from the "Templo de las Caritas" at Cempoala in Mexico have been interpreted by traditionalist scholars as symbols of the Sun and Moon. In that on the left it would not, however, be difficult to discern an instrument of navigation and in that on the right a space vehicle.

definitively, for many of them have their roots in a still more distant past. The tortured desire to abandon this planet does not, in all probability, refere to any aspiration for a life beyond the grave.

I look with hatred on death and I suffer . . .

says the singer, and continues:

It matters not what precious stones
The same thread unites,
It does not matter that we are united
Like gems on the same necklace . . .
My friend, my true friend,

Let us love one another, for the love of God.
As you know, so too do I know; we live only once.
One day we shall go hence.
We are come here only to know one another,
Only on loan have we come to the Earth . . .
Yet we live here with dejection,
Here, where we are watched and spied upon . . .[71] (13)

How could they not have been "watched and spied
upon," these foreigners who came from the unknown with
Fig. 200 "serpents of flame" and "birds of fire"? Feared and admired at the same time, their memory was to remain very
much alive throughout the millennia, not only in America,
but throughout the whole globe.

This memory is expressed by totem poles, by masks, by
graffiti and drawings, decorations and ornaments, even in
places and in times when the meaning of the symbols had
become lost or distorted.

This has not, however, happened among the Indians of
Fig. 201 Nootka Island (British Columbia, Canada), representatives
of a civilization at lease five thousand years old, over
whom still rises the flying figure with flaming wings, whose
Fig. 202 helmet-like mask decorates the chief of their dignitaries.

On Easter Island only a ritual, as significant as it is
ingenuous, has survived. It is carried out without any
memory of a very remote past which nevertheless has left
behind it many striking features. The monstrous bird-
men look down on us from the monoliths, reminding us
Fig. 203 of the enigmatic text of the "Table X": "The flying
men are coming . . . the men with the hats are flying . . ."[72]

Fig. 204 What hats? Perhaps that sort of helmet which seems to
cover the face of Makemake, the god who is also represented as flying.

On certain statues of this nightmare land, then, the
symbolic distortions are most varied, ranging from the
Fig. 205 enormous beaks to the "special" heads, and sometimes
accompanied by details which seem to be trying to remind

256

Fig. 200. The fabulous "firebird" dominating a totem pole of the Nootka Indians.

us of space suits even though traditional science is of another opinion.

The beaks of some of these Easter Island birds approximate to the forms of the "sacred hornbills" of New Guinea, but are always accompanied by the solar symbol. Logically more elaborate are the representations of the great Mediterranean civilization. But here too the Sun is frequently present: in the eyes or on the head of Horus, the Egyptian falcon-god, stylized in the flowers of "the tree of life" (which a winged divinity with the head of a bird of prey is sprinkling with lustral water in a Mesopotamian relief), or represented, together with the Moon, between Zeus Lykaios and his eagle.

At 2,650 meters (8,745 ft.) above sea level, in the chain of the High Atlas, in the region of Oukaimeden (southern Morocco), Willy Fassio has taken photographs of numerous carvings, which date back to prehistory, showing bird-headed axes.

So far so good, but similar weapons have been found portrayed in the Valley of Marvels. The photo (courteously supplied by an enthusiast from the National Institute of Ligurian Studies, Enzo Bernardini, to whose important labors we shall return later) leaves no further doubt. And in these weapons are mirrored, very probably, the "scepters" found in Europe which go back to Magdalenian times. No one knows what purpose they served; scientists are, however, unanimous in regarding them as "batons of command," magic symbols of power.

Surely we must suspect here some affinity with the mythical "bird of fire"? One can see it clearly in that Celtic "owl" discovered at Bra in eastern Jutland, so similar to the sinister American carvings.

It would be hazardous to establish similar links with the very beautiful Visigothic brooches of gold and precious stones, but the allure of ancient Egypt and ancient Mexico is too powerful not to favor fantastic speculations, nourished by the solar and stellar symbols placed on the breasts of those marvellous birds made men.

Fig. 206

Fig. 207

Fig. 208

Fig. 209

Fig. 210

Fig. 211

Fig. 212

Fig. 213

258

Fig. 201. A Nootka helmet reproduces in an astonishing manner the head of a mythical bird.

Fig. 202. The mysterious "bird-men" of the Easter Island monoliths.

Fig. 203. The Easter Island god Makemake in his "spacial mask." The face seems to be enclosed in a helmet.

Now look at Vishnu mounted on his sacred flying Garuda, just as his divine colleagues sat at the controls of that murderous aerial means of destruction, the *Vimâna*.

In *Shadows on the Stars* we referred to the mandarin who, about 1500, tried without great success to make a chest designed by himself rise into the skies by using rockets. We can now add that he had precursors whose exploits were crowned with greater success: the Chinese Emperor Shun, who reigned 4,200 years ago, was one of the first pilots recorded in ancient chronicles . . . and even the first parachutist, given that he seems to have invented a device similar to that which is being used at present.[73]

Was flight really known in antiquity?

"In a poem entitled *Li Sao*," according to a Chinese review, "Chu Yuan (340–278 B.C.) tells us of an aerial voyage over Asia. He states that as he knelt before the tomb of the Emperor Shun there appeared "a jade chariot drawn by a four dragons." Chu Yuan mounted the chariot

Fig. 214

Fig. 204. Other "spacial" figures from Easter Island; the symbolic distortions are very striking and numerous.

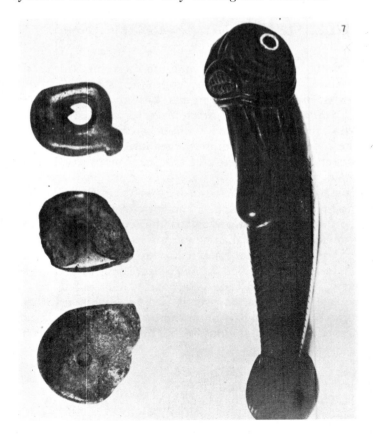

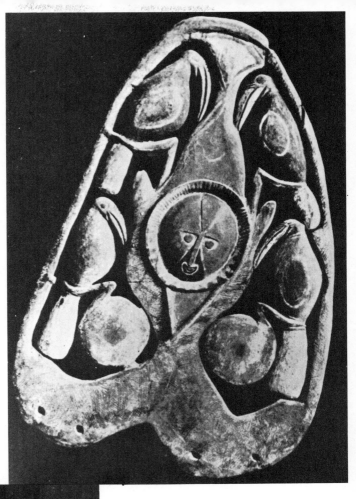

Fig. 205. Sacred birds
and solar symbols of
New Guinea.

263

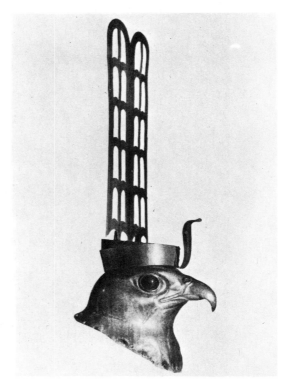

Fig. 206. The Egyptian falcon-god Horus from Hiero-
compolis (Ancient Empire).

Fig. 207. (Opposite page, above) A Mesopotamian relief
of the ninth century B.C. A winged genie with an eagle's
head waters the "tree of life."

Fig. 208. (Opposite page, below) Zeus Lykaios with the
eagle and stellar signs.

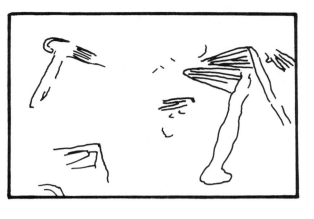

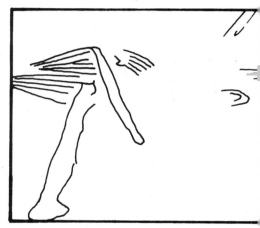

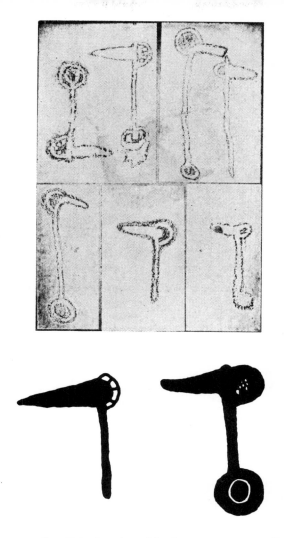

Fig. 210. Graffiti showing "beak axes" extraordinarily similar to those found in Morocco. These were found in the Valley of Marvels (Alpes Maritimes).

Fig. 209. (Opposite page) Drawing showing bird-headed axes found at 2,650 meters (8,745 ft.) above sea level in the High Atlas mountains (southern Morocco) by the explorer Willy Fassio.

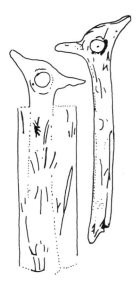

and flew at a great height across China in the direction of the Kun Lun mountains. During this voyage he was able to observe the earth without being troubled either by the winds or by the sands which whirled over the Gobi desert. He touched down without incident and later had another occasion to fly over the Kun Lun." [74]

"The flying machines of ancient China," Andrew Tomas remarks, "were either a product of scientific experimentation or a memory from a precataclysmic race. As the Chinese had no technology at the time, there is no alternative but to accept the second possibility . . .

"In the twelfth year of the Emperor Yao's reign (2346 B.C.) a strange man appeared. His name was Chih Chiang Tzu-yu. He was so skilful an archer that the Emperor named him 'Divine Archer' and appointed him 'Chief Mechanician.'

"In the annals of Chinese history he is reported to have ridden a 'celestial bird.' When 'carried into the center of an immense horizon' he noticed that he could no longer

Fig. 212. This Celtic "owl" found at Bra in eastern Jüt-
land very closely resembles certain sinister monuments
of pre-Columbian America.

Fig. 213. Two marvellous Visigothic brooches showing
birds with astral symbols on their breasts.

observe the rotary movement of the sun. In space, beyond the earth, our astronauts are also unable to see the sun rise or set."

Another Peking monthly reminds us that the great Chinese thinker Chuang Tzu wrote in the third century before our era a work entitled *Travel to the Infinite* which tells how he was taken up into space to 53,000 kilometers (84,800 mi.) from the earth on the back of "a fabulous bird of enormous dimensions." [75]

Professor Roerich in the course of his wanderings through Mongolia and Tibet heard talk of "iron serpents" which in ancient times "devoured space with fire and smoke," "reaching as far as the distant stars." And, he asserts, he found confirmation of these tales in some old Buddhist books.[76]

Let us give an account of the strange stone discs found in the district of Baian-Kara-Ula, apparently similar in shape to present-day phonograph records. Professor Tsum Um-Nui of the Academy of Prehistory of Peking believes that he has deciphered numerous inscriptions on them; and these appear so sensational that the Institute itself (after comprehensible hesitation) gave to the press a report whose title sounds clear enough: *Disc Hieroglyphics Speak of Spaceships 12,000 years ago.*

"Nothing is lost on this earth," writes Ivar Lissner, "No light is extinguished forever. Immortality is the sole reality which still emerges from the dust, from the ruins, from the destruction. For that reason no one lives in vain. For that reason whatever one thinks is not useless. For that reason not an hour is wasted. For that reason everything is united, in some place. And once again begins its activity."

Fig. 214. (Preceding page) Vishnu riding on the sacred Garuda bird; this wooden sculpture from Bali has its counterpart in many masterpieces of Indian religious art.

VIII

Thunderbolts and Atomic Force

John Clark dressed in the only garments at his disposal, buckled on his pistol belt, picked up his sten gun, the sack containing the objects which were of the most use to him, and made his way to the clearing. He already knew what awaited him there; the long daily morning discussion, a conversation which certainly would be useful to him, since it brought him, day by day, a deeper knowledge of the language of the natives, their mentality, their customs, but which had begun to bore him because of its nature which had long become a sort of rite.

As he took his place among the warriors squatting in a circle, the elder of the tribe greeted him:

"May you have good hunting again today, white god."

"And may you also be granted good hunting, brothers."

From the pile of food brought to him, John Clark rejected the badly cooked meat and chose some fruit. He thought of a good cup of coffee or tea, dreamed of a cigarette, and prepared to face the morning interrogation with the usual questions and the usual replies which he hoped every time to make a little clearer to his hosts. He had flown away on a jet from a brutal war, resolved to find some refuge from that inferno, and had dropped there, just where the jungle had swallowed up forever many men too reckless, incautious or unfortunate.[77]

"White god, where are your wings?"

272

"I have told you, I have no wings. I am a being such as you are."

"You are not as we are. You arrived flying."

"Very well, something made me fly, but . . ."

"Then you are a bird."

"I am not a bird. My plane, my machine . . ."

John Clark stopped, aware that to these primitive warriors words like "plane" or "machine" made no sense.

"It is like an animal," he tried to explain, "an animal made of . . . well, of iron."

"Iron," the elder of the tribe nodded gravely. "An iron serpent with wings."

"No, no. Another kind of animal. Think of any sort of animal that can fly."

"It lives on Earth, but can fly," the other made a gesture of grave assent. "It is like Waba, the stone monster which stays on the mountain and gives birth to the thunder, the lightning and the rain."

"No, not like that! I . . ."

"You came with the thunder and the lightning. You are master of the thunder and the lightning."

At that point the white man no longer knew what to reply. He understood that, for the natives, the roar and flames of the jet, the fire of his automatic weapons, were irrefutable arguments.

"Just as you like," he muttered resignedly in his own language.

The native perhaps interpreted these words as a magic spell and once again nodded in satisfaction.

"Waba has feet as powerful as yours," he remarked, indicating the aviator's boots, "and his stamping raises the thunder. He has great eyes of lightning and brilliant feathers as shining as your wings . . ."

The "great eyes" were the eye-pieces of Clark's helmet and the "brilliant feathers" his flight-dress. The elder touched it with interest and reverence and then, after thinking out the question, asked:

Fig. 215. The "Teotihuacán warrior" in his strange helmet with eyeholes, a sort of overall and unusual boots. Specialists cannot agree about the sort of weapons he holds in his hands.

Fig. 216. Probably a priest of Teotihuacán; his clothing abounds in cosmic symbols.

Fig. 217. At the center of the Mexican "universal cross," rich in striking symbolism, is the god of fire, with unknown weapons and thunderbolts hurled in all directions.

"Why don't your brothers and sisters too descend to us, he who shines by day and she who shines by night and has horns?"

He obviously meant the Sun and the Moon in its various phases. The white man, who had no difficulty in understanding, replied:

"They are in the heavens."

"You too were in the heavens," replied the other. "You descended from heaven. Why don't they descend?"

"Because they have work to do, up there. They must

give us warmth and light," concluded the aviator, rising; and added without the others understanding: "And we too, fellows, must get to work. Here we must work, if we want to live a little more decently."

An uneasy paradise

In this story only the name is fictitious. It was that of an American aviator which, for obvious reasons, we have changed. Let us imagine that we too have come into contact, as he did, with savages whose speech we understood only with difficulty and to whom certain objects were absolutely unknown. How could we hope to make clear to them conceptions like "machine," "plane," "helmet," to say nothing of jets or automatic weapons?

When handing down the story of the "white god," they would try, progressively, to symbolize it. They would represent, more or less clearly, certain of his attributes but others would become falsified, confused, adapted to their primitive ideas.

Had he lived in another epoch and another continent, John Clark might perhaps have been immortalized as the so-called "warrior of Teotihuacan," with his strange helmet which seems provided with eye-pieces, his shield and his bizarre implements which scholars have tried, with uncertainty and doubt, to see as arrows and a scepter (could they not be, instead, unknown weapons? less traditional scholars have asked themselves), his heavy and very elaborate footwear, in which we seem to discern the laces, and an overall recalling, without too great an effort of the imagination, a spacesuit with lines similar to jets of flame?

The cloak of another personage of Teotihuacán, presumably a priest, is more ceremonial but several details recall those of the "warrior" and it abounds in stellar symbols.

The very beautiful "universal cross" of the ancient Mexicans abounds in "astronautical" allusions. In the center

Fig. 215

Fig. 216

Fig. 217

276

Fig. 218. The "paradise of Tlaloc"; men with tongues of fire which make one think of propulsion jets seem to hover in space.

of the "celestial zones" is the god of fire, he too with a sort of helmet, unknown weapons and thunderbolts, launched towards the four cardinal points.

The symbolism surrounding him is impressive: "trees of life" surmounted by the "solar parrot," different in each branch of the cross, born of a wind-rose, arid, flowery, transformed into flaming stems, into flaming serpents, into serpent-birds, into reptiles flying among volutes, which are themselves bursts of flame, pursued by eagles, and creatures, some human, some monstrous and some made unrecognizable by what the more daring researchers persuade us to call "space masks."

The design lends itself to the most astonishing interpretations in every detail, so much so indeed as to justify those who have called it "a compendium of pre-Columbian science fiction."

Fig. 218   It would not be out of place to apply the same definition to the so-called "Paradise of Tlaloc," a Mexican mural in which men, emitting tongues of flame which make one think of jet propulsion, seem to hover in space among "moths," "discs," "goblets" and indefinable objects. Allusions to spirals abound, and there is even the sign 8, symbol of the infinite!

In the lower section there is a whole swarm of symbols, at the center of which stands out, straining skyward, a splendid "tree of life."

Fig. 219   Translated into different images, there is an analogous scene on a stele of the Mesopotamian civilization of Ur (Ur Nammu), which goes back approximately to 2100 B.C. The idea of ascent is expressed here by a ladder; it leads upwards towards mysterious personages, some of whom are clustered around the omnipresent "tree of life."

Fig. 220   At the top the "sovereign" renders homage to the Sun and Moon; the waxing moon, represented at Nimrud, capital of the Assyrian kings, with its horns (and the solar disc) is placed on the head of a winged "priestess."

Let us go back to the North American totem poles, surmounted by a figure with outstretched wings. The son of the famous explorer Colonel Fawcett, lost in Amazonia, presents us, to illustrate a chapter of his book,[78] with a

Fig. 221   victorious winged warrior with the symbols of the Sun and of the serpent, his head enclosed with a circular structure; it is a figure extraordinarily similar to those of the ancient Mediterranean civilizations reproduced in *Not of This World* (facing page 225): In the Egyptian tomb

Fig. 222   of Seti I of the fourteenth dynasty, Isis, with arms outstretched, unfolds her wings in a pose which we would clearly call "totemic."

God-man-bird: the concept is very ancient, the juxtapo-

Fig. 219. (Opposite page) On this stele from Ur ladder signifies ascent to the skies where the "k renders homage to the stars.

sition so logical as to be common to the whole globe at all times. How otherwise could one represent a creature descended from the skies?

Fantasies common to every people? Possibly. However, the motifs which inspired them must have been common to them. It is too easy and in no way convincing to rely on the idea of a "magic mold, spontaneous and universal."

We can provide innumerable examples. A few juxtapositions, other than those already mentioned, should suffice to confirm bewildering theories. Let us look, for example, at the winged Etruscan geni of the sepulcher of the Volumni at Perugia, at the very beautiful Victory of Velleja (Piacenza). Here the wings are of stone; but they are the same feathers, turned to stone, of the picture of the Mexican "warrior" of Tlaxcala. His curious clothing makes us think of an overall, the belts that cross his chest clearly serve to support the great plumed mane on his back. And what sort of "knapsack" is it, placed between the spine and the wings? Whatever it may be (there are various interpretations), it is by no means unreasonable that some should see in it the ingenuous reproduction of a fuel tank or a propellor.

The helmet of our "warrior" is also crowned with plumes, as too the one on the head of a personage immortalized in a mural painting from the palace of Mari,[79] which could be confused, even by traditionalist scholars, with a headcovering of the ancient Mexicans.

It is transformed into a diadem of feathers among the Redskins and many Asian, African and Oceanic peoples. It becomes a winged crown for the Etruscans, with solar symbols, serpentiform volutes and spirals.

Wings for the infinite; suns sparkle in the eyes, on the sides, among the talons (and here they make us think of a symbol of conquest, of possession) of the sacred falcon Horus, just as they are mirrored in a golden necklace found at Byblos which dates from the second millenium B.C., when the kings of that flourishing center north of

Fig. 223

Fig. 224

Fig. 225

Fig. 226

Fig. 227

Fig. 228

280

Fig. 220. The winged priestess of Nimrud, with the lunar "horns" and the solar disc.

Tyre and Sidon were vassals of the Egyptians. Let us compare it with the figures on the Etruscan metal urn (*lebes*) found at Castelletto Ticino (Novara)[80] which is decorated with birds, griffins and serpents, and we shall have something to reflect upon.

Fig. 229

The central figure is that of a winged being with a human face. God-man-bird; this image dominates the whole past of the third planet, still accompanied by solar symbols, spirals and animal figures in Mesopotamia (Lagash, "Plaque of the priest Dudu," about 3000 B.C.), translated into talons, jaws, plumes, appendages which are at the same time tails, reptiles, tongues of flame, on the shields of ancient Mexico.

Fig. 230

In this mythological "coyote" Taylor Hansen sees a transposition of the "divine birds" of Asia, perhaps of the Garuda, the sacred bird of Vishnu (see Fig. 214), whose mask is worn by the mongol shamans.

Fig. 231

But is it a bird? Andrew Tomas says: "The Indian *Pantachantra* contains a tale of how once upon a time six youths constructed a dirigible airship, called 'Garuda,' which could take off, land and fly in any direction. It was operated by an elaborate control system, producing even flight and perfect maneuvering."

"An animal which lives on Earth, but can fly": how can one clothe a similar conception in images? Only by figures which synthetize it, rendering the ideas of speed, of power, of ability to raise itself from the earth. Flying lions, bulls and horses fuse attributes proverbial for millennia and together confuse the impressions of a still more remote past.

On a golden pin of the fifth century B.C. from the Black Sea, the Scythians combine a sea horse (perhaps a symbol of the deluge, of the unleashed power of the waters) with a winged and beaked horse. At Tiryns winged monsters, under the solar symbol, between "trees of life" render homage to a goddess who has standing behind her a falcon as protector.

Fig. 232

Fig. 233

Fig. 221. The South Aerican warrior drawn by Colonel Fawcett's son; symbols of the sun and the serpent are evident. His head is enclosed in a circular structure.

Fig. 222.The very beautiful Isis from the tomb of Seti I.

283

Fig. 223. The winged genii from the sepulcher of the
Volumni (Perugia).

Fig. 234

Fig. 235

Fig. 236

The Etruscans grafted the head of a "goatlike bird" on
to the back of a lion with a serpentiform tail in the
"chimaera" found at Arezzo in 1553 and restored by
Benvenuto Cellini and show us warriors fighting against
griffins beneath solar and serpentiform symbols in the
Hypogeum of the Volumni.

A plaque of beaten gold from Ziwiye in the north of
Mesopotamia offers us, finally, a bewildering compendium;

284

Fig. 224. The Victory of Velleja (Piacenza).

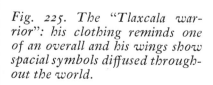

Fig. 225. The "Tlaxcala warrior": his clothing reminds one of an overall and his wings show spacial symbols diffused throughout the world.

285

wings, wings and yet more wings on animal bodies with beaked human, equine, faunlike, staglike heads, with tails of serpents or of feathers, they too surrounded by Suns and "trees of life."

Fig. 237 What is the matrix of this surprising explanation of symbolic images? The "sphinx of Monte Albán" perhaps, that hallucinatory figure, clinging to the rock as if in a desperate attempt to scale it, just as Waba, the "stone monster" of New Guinea, which stays on the mountain and gives birth to thunder, lightning and rain?

Fire all around

"Ea, lord of knowledge and wisdom, once decided as a jest to create a being who would have the appearance of a man and the wisdom of the gods," writes Gaster, evoking a Babylonian myth.[81] "He therefore came down to Earth and in the sacred city of Eridu gave form to a being to whom he gave the name Adapa. So wise was this being that nothing, either in heaven or on Earth, could escape his understanding. When he opened his mouth it was as if the gods themselves spoke and no one could contradict his words. There was no art or skill of which he was not the master. He knew how to knead bread like a baker, to fish like a fisherman and to hunt like a hunter. And he was as good as he was wise.

"One day, having gone out to look for fish for Ea, he met by chance the spirit of the hurricane, *which appeared in the form of a bird* and overturned his boat. Adapa hurled an imprecation against the bird, whose wings broke to pieces.

"Thus the wind which the bird had aroused on Earth ended. God then ordered that Adapa be brought before him. Following the advice of Ea, Adapa behaved humbly, so God pardoned him and said: "Adapa, even though you must now return to Earth, nonetheless I will reward you . . ."

"And God revealed to him all the secrets of the heavens

286

Fig. 226. (Opposite page) This personage immorta in a painting in the palace of Mari on the Euph wears a plumed helmet somewhat similar to those o ancient Mexicans.

Fig. 227. The Etruscan "winged crowns," together with spirals, serpentiform volutes and solar symbols.

Fig. 228.The splendid Horus falcon of Byblos.

Fig. 229. An Etruscan lebes *(metal urn) found in the province of Novara has in its center a winged figure surrounded by birds, griffins and serpents.*

and all his glory and splendor, conceding him great privileges, such as immunity from sickness and from pain."

It is really not difficult to translate the Babylonian story into science-fiction terms. The administrator of the globe Alpha, belonging to the Delta interplanetary federation, decided to send to Earth, as the leader of a colonizing mission, commandant Adapa. The operation was successful and Alpha's envoy managed to impart to the natives those ideas indispensable for their ascent. However, another cosmic vehicle violated the air-space of the third solar planet. Adapa "broke its wings to pieces," that is to say brought it down without knowing that it was a spaceship of the federation. The crash provoked a standstill in the evolution of man, which was not at all to the taste of the head of the stellar coalition, who called on the person responsible to give an account of his actions. Having assured himself of Adapa's good faith as well as of his impulsiveness, he did not condemn him, but destined him for another job; he would no longer lead space expeditions but would be exclusively employed in assisting the advancement of earthly men.

A very free interpretation? Certainly. It could, however, be supported by very many traditions analogous to the Babylonian ones. In India we find Indra, god of the tempest, who destroys the serpent, Vitra "by means of a thunderbolt, amid the thunders which were the roaring of the god and the lightning flashes which shook the mountains"; in Burma we meet Puluga, the supreme being, who "has the thunder for voice and the wind for breath" and who comes down to Earth to bring prosperity to man. In Nigeria, M'scimba-M'sciamba "sets fire to and shakes the world" in order later to induce men to make the soil fertile; among the Aztecs the goddess of the maize (and therefore of food, of life) was called "Seven Serpents" and, under the classic solar symbols, grasps the thunderbolt. For the ancient Lithuanians the supreme deity was Perkunas "the true celestial being, conceived in the form of

Fig. 238

290

Fig. 230. A Mesopotamian plaque of about 3000 B.C., with wings, spirals, solar symbols and lions, reproduces in a different style many very ancient American concepts.

Fig. 231. The Mexican "bird-coyote." Perhaps it is a transposition of analogous Asiatic mythological figures?

Fig. 232. On a Scythian gold pin a sea horse (symbol of the Deluge?) faces a winged and beaked horse.

Fig. 233. Tiryns: winged monsters under the solar symbol render homage to a goddess who has behind her a protector in the form of a falcon.

Fig. 234. In the "Etruscan chimaera" restored by Benvenuto Cellini, a "goat-bird" is grafted onto the back of a lion with a serpentiform tail.

Fig. 235. Warriors fighting with griffins in the Hypo-geum of the Volumni.

Fig. 236. The enigmatic winged figures from Ziwiye in northern Mesopotamia.

Fig. 237. The "sphinx of Monte Albán," a bewildering figure.

a meteorite, that is to say a provoker of thunder and lightning. He was given the epithets proper to the Supreme Being: father (*téras*) and ancestor (*duojotas*). Fire is the element which represents him . . . he is pictured as a mature man with flames on his head . . ." [82]

The Mexican Quetzalcoatl, in the picture in the *Codex Fiorentino* (see Fig. 50), also has "flames on his head" and the Indian god of fire, Agni, whose manifestations are both in the Skies (with the Sun and the lightning) and on Earth, is sometimes pictured in a similar way. "He," Turchi writes, "is everywhere, in the heart of the stone, in the entrails of the earth, within our own bodies . . . He is the friend of men, because he puts to flight the evil spirits which lurk in the shadows and consumes them in his heat, and grants to men all the favors of the domestic hearth through the very ancient pact concluded with our ancestors . . ."

Readers will certainly recall the "Palenque astronaut," that surprising personage pictured on a Mexican tombstone. G. Tarade and A. Millou write of him: "The man portrayed is wearing a helmet and looking in the direction of the ship's prow; his hands are busy and appear to be working levers, while his head is resting on a support and he has an inhaler in his nose. The bird on the prow is a parrot which for the Maya was a Sun-God symbol. Also on the bows we find three 'receivers' for accumulating energy, and elsewhere inside the ship there are others, in groups of three. The motor is in four parts and the system propelling it is behind the pilot . . . in the back a jet of flame is clearly visible." [83]

Be as skeptical as you will, but it is impossible to find any interpretation for this relief other than a "special" one. At the time of its discovery a scholar peremptorily stated that it was a representation of the god of rain. The assertion is absolutely gratuitous, since official science is not in a position, even now, to identify this figure. It is based, however, on a very simple consideration; the divinity to whom has been attributed the power of unleashing the thunder and the lightning must logically also control all meteorological phenomena.

This happens in the Andaman Islands, where the god of thunder is also the god of rain, and it also occurs among the Denca of Central Africa, among the Nuba settled to the west of the white Nile, and among the Hottentots.

It happens also in India with Parjanya, god of the tempest and of rain, and at Ugarit with Baal, whose specific name was Hadad, "lord of the thunder, of the lightning, of the waters of heaven, he who rides upon the clouds."

Were we to search among these and other divinities with similar attributes for "special" characteristics, we would find them in profusion: the "solar fringes" on the strange headgear of the Aztec Chalchihuitlicue; the lateral protuberances found on many shaman masks (see Fig. 119); as well as the famous "dancer" with his supposedly astronautical helmet; we see in Valcamonica another very strange figure streaming rain upon the "trees of life." A profusion of drops surround the horned head of the so-called "white woman of Aouanrhet," a neighbor of the "Martians of Tassili." Drops seems to compose the "mythical figure of pluvial character" from northwest Australia, preserved in the Städtisches Völkermuseum at Frankfurt on Main. If anyone, making use of primitive techniques, tried to reproduce the outline of an astronaut, he would not be able to make a more suggestive one; from the "bands" (pectoral and abdominal) to the transparent helmet to something which might be an antenna, here symbolized by a feather.

Fig. 239

Fig. 240

Fig. 241

Fig. 242

Radioactive skeletons

In his right hand the "Australian astronaut" appears to be holding some implement of which, unfortunately, we cannot even reconstruct the shape. A weapon? We are

Fig. 239. (Above) Chalchihuitlicue, a divinity of ancient Mexico, has a "solar Fringe" on her unusual headdress.

Fig. 238. (Left) Lightning is the weapon of the Aztec goddess of maize (and therefore of food, of life), crowned by astral symbols.

297

tempted to tell once again the Canaanite myth about which Theodor Gaster writes:

"At the beginning of time, when to each of the gods his share of dominion was assigned, the Earth still did not have a master. Two gods contested the honor: one was Baal, *lord of the air and the rain*, the other was Yam, the dragon that reigned over the waters. The dominion was entrusted to Yam, but Baal challenged him. Astarte aided Baal and made him two 'magic cudgels' with which he conquered and killed the dragon." Commenting on the legend, Gaster continues: "This episode recurs in an Egyptian myth which describes the contest between Horus and Set. It says, in fact, that Horus was armed with a special weapon made by Ptah, the armorer of the gods. In a similar way in the Vedic myths, when Indra attacks the dragon Vritra, he is armed with a '*whistling javelin*' expressly made for him by the craftsman Tvashtri. Students of mythology, generally speaking, agree in admitting that *these arms represent the lightning.* Furthermore . . . in the original text it is said that the cudgels 'leapt' from the hands of Baal . . ."

When we remember how the primitive friends of John Clark associated the roar and the flames of the jet with the fire from the sten gun and the pistol, the words of Gaster assume a fresh significance.

What he tells of Baal, moreover, has echoes throughout the world. In Tibet, the *dorje* (lightning) is regarded as a weapon and is used symbolically by the priests against the demons.

The Soviet scholar Gorbovsky [84] has much material concerning celestial vehicles before the flood. Dealing especially with Tibet, he tells us that a Tibetan text contains the description of an "enormous flying wagon made of a black metal with an iron base, not drawn by horses or elephants but by machines as large as those animals."

Celtic traditions abound in descriptions of "flying animals covered with iron armor, which have neither bones

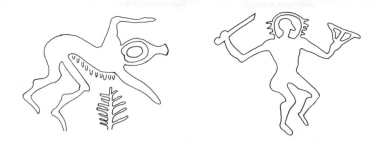

Fig. 240. Alongside the famous "Valcamonica spaceman" another very strange figure pours rain upon the "tree of life."

Fig. 241. The "white woman of the Tassili'," her horned head wreathed in droplets.

nor skeletons and which do not require food," whereas a flying machine is thus described in ancient India: "In the interior of the apparatus is an appliance where mercury is heated in a copper. The heating is obtained by a special flame capable of being directed (a laser?). The four mercury recipients together produce a whirlwind of power. The wagon rises into the sky with a crash like thunder. Those who follow its course in the sky have the impression of watching a gigantic pearl."

Once more Gorbovsky speaks: In his book *Riddles of Antiquity* he notes that "a human skeleton found in India revealed a radioactive content fifty times higher than normal" (it is not the only one, as we shall see). Referring to the carbonized ruins of Borsippa, often identified with those of the Tower of Babel, E. Zehren asks in his book *Die Biblischen Hügel* what sort of power could have melted the bricks of the ziggurat, and replies: "Nothing, except the monstrous flesh of an atomic bomb."

Sir Frederick Soddy, awarded the Nobel price in 1921 for his important discovery of isotopes, wrote in 1909 about the traditions handed down to us from prehistory: "Can we not read into them some justification for the belief that some former forgotten race of men attained not only the knowledge we have so recently won but also to the power that is not yet ours." The scientific traditions of antiquity could be the echo of prehistoric epochs in which man had already advanced along the same road.

Fig. 242. (Opposite page) Astronauts in Australia? Th *"pluvial figure" seems to confirm a science fiction hy* *pothesis.*

IX

Builders of Eternity

Lug, the veteran Earth astronaut, urgently summoned by the Interplanetary Council, listened patiently to the charges against him.

"You have misused our science, thus accelerating, in an unnatural manner, the evolution of the inhabitants of the globe which you have explored."

"I could not do otherwise. We had need of metal. I had to teach the natives how to extract it and work it in order to supply our own needs. We had need of wood; I had to provide them with the tools to cut it down and shape it. We had need of . . ."

"You," the interrogator interrupted him, "have handed our knowledge over to the natives."

"What else could I do? Cancel it from their memories? After having made them work for us? They certainly cannot use it to trigger off a war."

"You," continued the other, "were regarded as a sort of magician by these natives."

"If you were a primitive and had an attack of fever and I made it disappear with a little pill, you, too, would consider me a magician."

"Be that as it may, you are aware that you have broken the rules of the Council?"

"Yes, sir," Lug the astronaut began to lose patience. "I did so out of necessity, because I believed it just and opportune, and I have no intention of making excuses. Go to

Earth yourself next time and just see if you can find a way out, dancing the tightrope with your quibbles."

"Commandant," burst out the inquisitor, but suddenly had second thoughts, sat down again and muttered: "The devil with it! It is always the same with this fellow; not once have we been able to clip his wings."

Then he announced, loudly and reluctantly: "The meeting is closed. The record will be placed in the files."

Eternal lamps

Here is another little science fiction story which might provide a spacial key to the legend, or indeed to a whole series of legends.

In the Irish sagas Lug is the engineer, the builder, the magician; he is the doctor and alchemist. He is the universal craftsman and, as such, has different personalities. He is the demiurge, the creator, the son of Cian or Gian, "the Flaming One." He is the son of Lir or Leir, he is the son of Dian Cecht, and as such he is carpenter, smith, athlete, harpist, warrior, poet, magician, physician, cup-bearer, bronze-worker, chess champion. He will be the spiritual father of Cuchulain.[85] In Scandinavia he is Loki, a sort of demon among the gods, and becomes "the crafty one," "the ingenious," he who deceives the other gods.[86]

However closely the Utopian version fits our case, we certainly do not want to take it for granted. It should simply make us reflect on certain facts which are inexplicable in the present state of our knowledge.

"In the Sactaya Grantham, which belongs to the Vedas of India," writes Andrew Tomas, "there are directions for vaccination and a description of its effects. How did the Brahmins make this discovery in biology some 4,000 years before Jenner?"[87]

And he adds something even more sensational: "Did the ancient Chinese have the X-ray? The question may seem absurd in the extreme, yet Emperor Tsin Shi (259-210 B.C.) did have a mirror which "would illuminate the bones of the body." The mirror was located in the palace at Hien-Yang in Shensi in 206 B.C., and contemporary writings represent it as follows: "It was a rectangular mirror 4 feet wide, 5 feet 9 inches high, brilliant both on its outer and inner sides. When a man stood straight before it to see his reflection, his image appeared reversed. When someone placed his hands on his heart, he observed his five viscera placed side by side and not impeded by any obstacle. When a man had a hidden malady within his organs, he could recognize the root of his complaint by looking into this mirror and laying his hands on his heart." [88]

It seems that two hundred and fifty years before the reign of Tsin Shi a Hindu sage called Jivaka possessed a "marvellous jewel" which made it possible to "look at the inside of the body," just like X-rays. This object, according to a historical document, "illuminated the body as a lamp lights up all objects in a house, and so revealed the nature of the malady."

More modest inventions, but nonetheless surprising to us, can be found in the "minor" pages of archaeology. In the "Ballana tomb" on the Nubian Nile, for example, was discovered an extremely practical folding table, and a similar one was found at Pompeii. Another excursion into the past reveals a seat, it too folding, but for this we shall have to cover a considerable distance. We find it in Denmark, fashioned about three thousand years ago.

A very strange segmented box, similar to those in which we keep cutlery today, was found in a tomb of ancient Egypt, dating back to about 3000 B.C. And now at last we know how the perfect cut of the moustaches of Prince Rahotep (about 2500 B.C.) was obtained. "During an excavation season in the Sakkara region," we read in a newspaper, "the American Egyptologist Walter Emery

Fig. 243

Fig. 244

Fig. 245

Fig. 246

Fig. 243. (Opposite page, above) A folding bronze ta▮ from Ballana (Nubian Nile). When opened (on rig▮ the legs support a wooden tray.

Fig. 244. (Opposite page, below) Another folding pi▮ of furniture: a Danish seat from 3000 B.C.

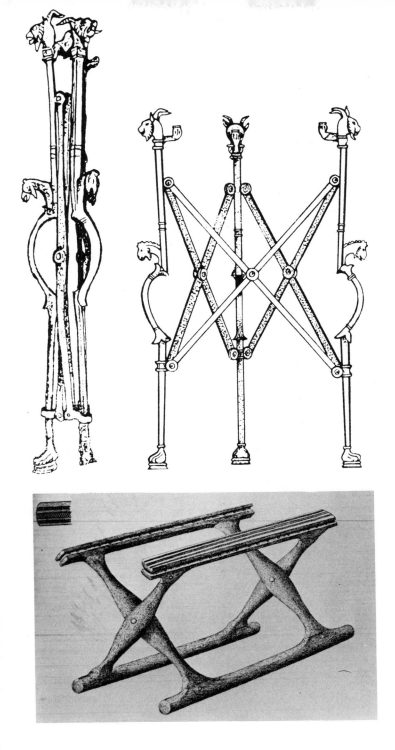

and the Egyptian archaeologist Aliel Kholi found eleven rusted razor blades, 4,500 years old. Emery and el Kholi now want to remove the rust from them in order to read the hieroglyphics on the blades." [89]

We have not yet got as far as electric razors, but we should not despair, considering the discovery by the German engineer Wilhelm König of the famous "Baghdad dry cell batteries." [90]

Electricity should not, however, be regarded as a prerogative of the Mediterranean world. An ancient Hindu manuscript, the *Agastya Samhita,* preserved in the Princes' Library at Ujjain, contains detailed instructions for the construction of an electric dry-cell battery: "A well-cleaned copper plate should be placed in an earthenware vessel. It should then be covered first by copper sulphate and then by moist sawdust. A mercury-amalgamated zinc plate to prevent polarization should then be placed on the

Fig. 245. This tray with compartments, extraordinarily similar to those of our own times, was found in an ancient Egyptian tomb and dates from more than 3000 B.C.

Fig. 246. The perfect moustaches of the Egyptian prince Rahotep have at last been explained by the recent find of razor blades in an ancient Egyptian tomb.

top of the sawdust. By their contact a liquid energy known by the twin name of Mitra-Varuna is produced. Water is split up by this current into Pranavayu and Udanavayu. The joining together of one hundred of such vessels is said to be very active and effective." [91]

Commenting on this passage, Tomas gives us an interesting summary of the supposed knowledge of electricity in the distant past.

"Ovid writes that Numa Pompilius, the second king of Rome, used to invoke Jupiter to light altars by flames from the sky. Numa caused a perpetual light to burn in the dome of a temple which he had built. Pausanias observed a golden lamp in the Temple of Minerva in A.D. 170. It provided illumination for a year without refuelling.

"Among the tombs near Memphis, the ancient city of Egypt, ever-burning lights have been found in sealed chambers, but after exposure to air the flames went out. Similar perpetual lamps are known to have existed in the Brahmin temples of India.

"The statue of Memnon in Egypt spoke as soon as the rays of the rising sun fell upon its mouth. The sound came from the base of the figure. In the words of Juvenal: 'Memnon sounds his magic strings.' The Incas had a speaking idol in the valley of Rimac. Needless to say, the construction of these statues required a knowledge of physics.

"There are reasons to believe that flashes from the eyes of Egyptian gods, particularly those of Isis, could have been produced by electricity, since strange appliances have been found in Egypt.

"Lucian (A.D. 120-180), the Greek satirist, made a trip to Hierapolis in Northern Syria and described its marvels. He saw a gem on the goddess Hera's head from which flashed a great light—'so that the whole temple gleams brightly as by the light of myriads of candles.' There was also another wonder. The eyes of Hera followed a person no matter where he moved. Lucian did not explain the phenomena because he could not—the priests kept him in the dark about their science."

Turning to other strange instances Tomas continues: "The colorful frescoes on the walls and ceilings of rock-cut tombs in Egypt must have been painted in bright light. However, daylight never reaches these dark chambers. There are no stains from oil lamps or torches. Were electric lights employed in some of them? [92]

"The mysteries of the Temple of Hadad or Jupiter at Baalbek were connected with luminous stones. The existence of these stones, providing a source of lighting at night in ancient times, cannot be questioned because so many classical writers describe them.

"Plutarch wrote in the first century of our era that he had seen a 'perpetual lamp' in the temple of Jupiter-Amun and that the priests assured him it had been burning continuously for many years. Neither wind nor water could extinguish it. A stone sepulcher of Pallas, the son of Evander, was found in 1401. At the head of the Roman stood a lamp burning with perpetual fire. . . . St. Augustine (b. A.D. 354) describes an ever-burning lamp he saw at the temple of Venus. Kedrenus (Cedrinus), eleventh-century historian of Byzantium, affirms that he observed a perpetual lamp at Edessa, Syria, where it had burnt for five hundred years.

"The Abbé Evariste-Régis Huc (1813-60) claimed that he had examined one of the perpetually burning lamps in Tibet.

Tales of strange lamps come to us from the Americas as well. In 1601 Barco Centenera wrote about the city of Gran Moxo near the source of the Paraguay River in the Mato Grosso. In this account he draws a picture of a mysterious island city from the reminiscences of conquistadores: "In the middle of the lake was an island on which were buildings of great beauty and splendor, beyond human understanding. The mansion of the Lord, the Gran Moxo, was built of white stone right to the very roof. It had two very high towers at its entrance, and a stairway in the middle. In the middle of a pillar, on the right, were two live lions (jaguars? A.T.). They couched at its sides,

in chains, whose links were made of gold. On the summit of this pillar, 25 feet high, was a great moon. It illuminated all the lake, dispelling darkness and shadows by night and day, so that all appeared very bright."

Colonel P. H. Fawcett was told by the natives in the Mato Grosso that mysterious cold lights had been seen by them in the lost cities of the jungle. Writing to Lewis Spence, the British author, he says: "These people have a source of illumination which is strange to us; in fact they are a remnant of civilization which has gone and which has retained old knowledge."

"Mandans, the white Indians of North America, remember an age when their ancestors lived in "cities with inextinguishable lights" beyond the ocean. Was it Atlantis? Is it from Atlantean survivors that the ancients inherited these strange lamps?

"Only a few decades ago Torres Strait islanders were known to have had 'booya' or round stones which emitted piercing light. . . . Greenish blue light, which would rise to a considerable distance, was a complete puzzle to the white men who saw a 'booya.' [93]

"A few years ago traders in New Guinea discovered a jungle valley near Mount Wilhelmina populated by amazons. They were terrified to see stone balls, about 12 feet in diameter mounted on columns, radiate neon-like light. C. S. Downey, a delegate to the conference on street lighting and traffic in Pretoria, South Africa, was so much impressed by the weird but effective form of illumination in this jungle in New Guinea, that he stated in 1963: 'These women, cut off from the rest of mankind, may have perfected a system of artificial illumination equal, if not superior, to the twentieth century.' It is most unlikely that the jungle amazons could have evolved a system of lighting superior to ours. It is more probable that they have inherited the incandescent spheres from a civilization of which there is no record in our histories."

It is a strange fact that an island peopled by women

g. 247. (Opposite page) According to traditional sci-ce, the ancient Mexicans were ignorant of the wheel, t the craftsmen of Vera Cruz, of Campache and of rasco have bequeathed us these toys with far from imitive characteristics.

warriors should have been called by the Romans (from a Celtic root) a name equivalent to our word "Brazil," which means initially the rosy color of burning coal.

City of another world

Some bizarre allusions might lead us to think that the Aztecs were familiar with electricity.[94] The facts in our possession are not sufficient to allow us to confront the problem in scientific terms. It seems, however, of interest to report an item of news from Mexico City which has perhaps escaped the attention of many. The engineer David Esparza Midalgo has invented a calculator based on the Aztec and Maya systems. The announcement was made in the daily paper *Novedades*. The machine is capable of carrying out all mathematical operations, including the extraction of cube roots, more rapidly than any modern machine.[95]

People who have reached such a level of achievement certainly cannot have been ignorant of the wheel. Yet it is a widely diffused belief, accepted by official science, that the wheel was totally unknown in "the new world." How are we to reconcile this with the Mexican wheeled toys from the Vera Cruz, Campeche and Tarasco cultures?

Fig. 247

Robert Calcagno provides us with extensive evidence of this; in his photos we see jaguars, dogs and other animals which can only be slightly identified, all of them resembling modern toys or puppets by their droll and witty expressions. "Carbon datings," states Tomas, "of these wheeled toys show that they are from 1,200 to 2,000 years old. The question still remains; why didn't the Mayas use vehicles if their children played with wheeled toys? After all, our kids play with toy cars because adults drive automobiles."

We let Gordon F. Eckholm reply: "The reason why the wheel was not used in America may be because it was not in widespread use in Asia either. The Paleoindians'

312

Fig. 248. Wheeled chariots in Saharan paintings. This is the so-called "two-horse chariot of Tin-Abu-Teka."

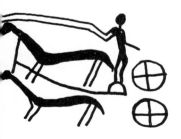

Fig. 249. This drawing on a slab from a burial chamber at Kivik in southern Sweden is very similar to that of the African chariot.

313

most common mode of transportation was the travois, a device consisting of two shafts attached by a belt to a dog's back. The ends of the shafts were left to trail along the ground. . ." [96] This method was later used by the Redskins and the American colonists.

The wheel, in fact, would have been not only superfluous but unsuitable, because of the nature of the ground to be covered. Surely that was why the wheel disappeared in the Sahara with the progressive drying-up of the soil, whereas the most ancient pictures of this area, which is now a desolate desert, show it as suitable for light horse-drawn carriages.

Fig. 248

Surprisingly similar to these African pictures is the carving in a sepulchral chamber of Kivik in southern Sweden, which we can see translated into a statuette about 1400-1200 B.C. at Trundholm in Denmark. The representations of chariots which so impress us, whether on the rocks of Los Buitres, Penalsordo (Badajoz, Spain) or on a shard from Sopron (Hungary), carry us back to the Sahara, Central Africa and Central Asia.

Fig. 249

Fig. 250

Fig. 251

Fig. 252

We do not pretend to see the permanent way of "prehistoric buses" in the mysterious cart-ruts of Malta, in some American centers or in the land of Mohenjo-Daro; but we must note that in the ruins of this last center there are features which astound us: houses of two or three stories provided with running water, very efficient sanitary services and a sewerage system which has made British experts say "We couldn't do better today!" [97]

Fig. 253

Nor can we, we hasten to add, build with such facility, complex monuments like those of so many regions of the ancient world. For example, the immense staircases of "Piedras Negras" in Guatemala or the Maya palaces of Sayil (Compeche), which seem to mirror, sometimes as a whole, sometimes only in detail, the masterpieces of Mediterranean building.

Fig. 254

Fig. 255

Such ruins have made possible a Mexican reconstruction

314

Fig. 250. The Danish "chariot of the Sun" from Trundholm (c. 1400-1200 B.C.)

Fig. 251. A "processional chariot" on a potsherd found at Sopron in Hungary.

Fig. 252. Calcolithic rock designs showing wheeled vehicles from Los Buitres, Penalsordo (Badajoz).

315

Fig. 253. A view of the perfect sewerage system of Mohenjo-Daro.

Fig. 254. (Opposite page, above) A reconstruction "Piedras Negras" in Guatemala.

Fig. 255. (Opposite page, below) The so-called "Pal. of the Maya city of Sayil (Campeche).

316

Fig. 256. The Mexican city of Tollan at its apogee; in the reconstruction there is something ultramodern and at the same time extraterrestial.

TOLLAN XICOCOTITLA
TULA DE ALLENDE. HIDALGO.

Fig. 256 of Tollan suggesting a sort of extraterrestial dream which overwhelms us.

Splendid buildings in perfect parallelopiped form, juxtaposed and superimposed, rise within an enormous open space, one side of which was entirely filled by a large covered square of astonishing dimensions. The imposing symbol of the step-pyramid dominates everything.

Fig. 257

Fig. 258 It is a symbol which is to be found everywhere,[98] from the impressive step-pyramid of Sakkara to the Chaldean temples and so many others that it seems to us unnecessary to make a list.

Fig. 259

Fig. 260 Let us mention, therefore, because of their enigmatic allusions, only a few such buildings, beginning with the so-called "Castillo" of Chichén-Itzá (Yucatan), which a very ancient tradition states was built over a "machine" of similar form capable of "travelling over great distances and for a very long time." Another legend tells us that under the Pyramid of the Moon of the beautiful and sinister Teotihuacán there sleeps in a crystal coffin a "blonde princess" who came from our natural satellite.

Fig. 261

Fig. 262 Still at Teotihuacán, as well as the lunar pyramid, there rises a pyramid dedicated to the Sun, whose details support the idea of close contact between the American and Egyptian civilizations. The dimensions of the base of the Mexican pyramid are similar to those of the pyramid of Cheops (225 x 220 m.) (742 x 726 ft.) and its height (73 m.) (240 ft.) is half that of the other.

Despite the accumulation of idiocies which have reached us from the so-called "pyramidologists," it is an undeniable fact that such buildings contain secrets which we are still far from understanding.

Fig. 263 Let us consider again the pyramid of Cheops; the "king's chamber" lies at the center of the circle formed by the vertices of the triangle, and the height of the pyramid itself corresponds to the radius of a circle whose circumference is equivalent to the perimeter of the base.

"Lobachevsky demonstrated the universality of space

Fig. 257. The Egyptian center of Sakkara with its famous step-pyramid must have looked like this.

Fig. 258. Reconstruction (according to Charles Chipiez) of a Chaldean temple which recalls the step-pyramid.

geometry," says Tomas. "This great science was somehow brought to the land of Egypt. But, by whom and from where? If the original 'Sons of the Sun' were culture-bearers from space, then many puzzles are solved. The universal science of geometry proves that life on other planets has probably appeared earlier but followed the same pattern in the field of knowledge as here on earth."

It might seem arbitrary to discern the fundamental concept of the pyramid in constructions which doubtlessly only resemble it in a vague manner. Numerous scientists, however, primarily Soviet ones, do not disregard certain definite affinities. They discern crude pyramidal bases in some primitive outlines of buildings on Easter Island (and Fig. 264 here we are back to the "Easter Island *nuraghi*" of lenticular form which strangely resemble certain French and Piedmontese finds, such as those of Val Gravio illustrated Fig. 265 in Fig. 123), and they find in spiral minarets reminiscences of the Mesopotamian ziggurats closely allied to the stepped monuments of Egypt and America.

The Huicol Indians of the "new continent" today still Fig. 266 build little step-pyramids of wood which they call "staircases of the Sun." Some of these have an extraordinary Fig. 267 similarity to the primitive Etruscan "canopes" [99] culminating in a sphere symbolizing a head.

Coming back to real pyramids, let us listen once more to Andrew Tomas:

"When pre-Inca stone masonry was uncovered at Ollantay-tambo and Sacsahuaman in Peru, the weight of some of the stones was estimated to be over 100 tons. In spite of their great mass, the blocks were put in place with such exactness that the joints could hardly be seen with the naked eye. No buildings anywhere in the world, except Egypt, have ever matched the architects of the magalithic structures of Peru.

"The Great or Khufu Pyramid of Egypt is one of the most accurate pieces of construction in the world. Its builders must have had a superior knowledge of geometry

Fig. 259. Chichén-Itzá (Yucatan): tradition has it that this monument was built over a "machine" capable of travelling in space and time.

and architecture. It has justly been said that 'Time laughs at everything, but the pyramids laugh at Time'.

"The fifteen-ton polished blocks at the base of the Khufu Pyramid are fitted together with an accuracy of one-hundredth of an inch. A thin piece of paper can scarcely be inserted between the blocks. Before our present technological century, no nation in history could duplicate such precision.

"If we accept the Egyptologists' date for the building of the Great Pyramid, then this structure, which has remained the highest on earth until recent times, was erected in an epoch when there were no cranes or even wheels. Only a century before the beginning of work on the pyramid, the Egyptians were still building in mudbrick. Are we then to believe that in one century the ancient Egyptians made so phenomenal an advance that it took them only twenty years to construct a stone edifice, the tallest until this century. . . ?

Fig. 260. The "Pyramid of the Moon "at Teotihuacán; under this building is said to sleep, in a crystal coffin, a legendary blonde princess.

Fig. 261. Still at Teotihuacán: the famous "Pyramid of the Sun."

Fig. 262. (Below) A surprising comparison; the Mexican "Pyramid of the Sun" and the Egyptian Pyramid of Cheops (outer triangle).

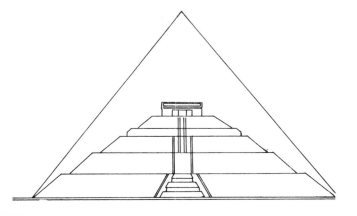

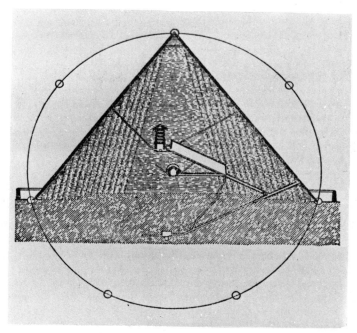

Fig. 263. The remarkable geometry of the Pyramid of Cheops according to accurate scientific research.

Fig. 264. This house of lenticular form from Eastern Island recalls both the nuraghi and the strange Piedmontese buildings of Val Gravio.

"The blocks of Baalbeck Terrace in Lebanon are fifty to a hundred times heavier than those of the Great Pyramid. Even gigantic cranes of today would be unable to raise them from the foot of the hill to the top on which the platform stands. . .

"François Lenormant, in his book on Chaldean Magic, cites a legend about the priests of On who could by means of sound raise into the air huge stones which a thousand men could not move. Is this only a myth or folk memory of the feats of a vanished science?"

In 1964 we wrote: "The American archaeologist A. Hyatt Verrill has put forward a still bolder hypothesis: he suggests that the stones of the pre-Columbian pyramids were not hewn by means of a chisel, but that the builders used a kind of radioactive paste which was capable of eating into granite. He claims to have seen for himself remnants of this substance in the possession of an Indian witch-doctor." [100]

Very well then. How would you propose to transport a stone that, even with the aid of many helpers, you could not succeed in moving an inch? In these days we could perhaps suggest the best method: break the mass into pieces, place the fragments in a type of "decoction" and you would see them transformed into blocks of malleable clay. Nothing would be easier, then, than to break up the blocks themselves to make them transportable, hand them over to your assistants and, once they had reached their destination, knead them into a whole. After a certain time they would again become stone, in the design which you found most opportune to give them.

A "decoction" which could soften rocks? Just that! On June 20 and 25, 1968, Italian Television reported its existence, adding that the vegetable components of this marvellous solvent had been discovered by an Italian missionary in Peru who had carried out experiments with complete success.

Rather than a discovery, it was a rediscovery; so the

Fig. 265. The mosque of Al-Mutawakkil with its spiral minaret brings to mind the Mesopotamian ziggurats.

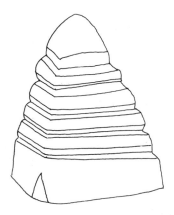

Fig. 266. The "stairway of the Sun" of the Huicol Indians of America.

missionary himself defined it, asserting that the Incas had made use of this solvent to construct their pyramids. If that was the case, the thought occurs that the solvent must have been known and used over a great part of the ancient world. In fact, the nature of the construction of the pyramids (they rise in Peru, in Mexico and Egypt) constitutes a puzzle which, notwithstanding many hypotheses, still remains to be solved.

As has been said, the massive blocks with which some of these monuments have been built must have been transported from distant places and often across pathless regions. To square blocks so heavy and to give to their sides a slightly conxev or concave form in such a way as to make them fit perfectly with the maximum guarantee of solidity poses another great problem. The arrangement of the blocks themselves even today would be a hard task for technicians. It would require, among other things, the use of reinforced concrete platforms able to support the weight of forty-wheeled railroad cars!

There has been, and still is, talk of inclined planes, of rollers made from tree trunks, but these are suppositions which are far from consistent. Such methods would not have been able to dispense with manpower. Let us admit that a thousand hands would not be enough to handle or to move one of these blocks; a thousend hands means five hundred men, for whom there would not have been room around the stone.

Being somewhat skeptical about Verrill's revelations, we are more inclined to think of lifting machines used by the Egyptians and the ancient Americans and then dismantled as the era of erecting cyclopean constructions came to an end. This, naturally, would only explain a part of the problem. The "rediscovery" of the missionary would, on the other hand, provide a complete solution to which no objections could be raised. But before becoming too enthusiastic, it seems to us reasonable to await further revelation.

The era of Gemini

According to the traditionalists, the Great Pyramid was constructed by the Pharoah Cheops of the fourth dynasty. There are some, however, of a different opinion. Among them, Richard Hennig who writes:

"There seems to be no reason why the majority of present-day Egyptologists, contrary to the opinions of many of their nineteenth century predecessors, should refuse with such obstinacy to date the history of ancient Egypt back to the fourth and fifth millennia b.c. The Babylonian civilization and that of the upper reaches of the Indus (to say nothing of the Maya) were already flourishing, it has been proved, roughly four to five thousand years before Christ.

"It is almost certain that the Maya traditions record celestial events from the ninth millennium b.c. Why shouldn't the Egyptian priests have had at their disposal equally ancient traditions to sustain their esoteric records? The Englishman Perry admits it and, in a recent text, dates the advent of the first Pharoah, Manes, as 4326 b.c.

"There exists, moreover, a hint by Herodotus (which he could certainly not have invented) on the remote period to which the knowledge of the Egyptian priests went back. They state," he writes, "that the Sun rose twice at the point where it now sets and set twice at the point where it rises today."

"It is clear that this refers to the phenomenon known as the 'precession of the equinoxes'. In effect our planet travels on an axis inclined to its orbit and the axis itself, directed from time to time towards successive points, returns to the 'position of departure' every 25,827 years.

"If Herodotus is to be taken literally, this would prove, therefore, that Egyptian astronomy covers fifty thousand years! Also, if the observation of the heavens by the priests of the Nile civilization did not have its beginnings in so remote a time, it necessarily extended over several mil-

329

lennia; otherwise it would not have been possible to calculate the precession. The Greeks discovered it in 150 B.C. The Babylonians, however, had some idea of it in earlier times, as they knew of astronomical phenomena which could have taken place only in the period called by convention the 'era of Gemini', that is from 6500 to 4300 B.C., when the constellation of Gemini coincided with the "spring point" of the solar year.

"Nothing hinders us from thinking that the Egyptians had achieved such knowledge thanks to a long observation of the starry sphere, the more so as the zodiac of the temple of Denderah, which dates from a few centuries before Christ, indicates exactly the Gemini as the symbol of spring. The only conclusion possible is that Egyptian astronomical science goes back at least to the 'era of Gemini.' And the idea of placing the construction of the Great Pyramid in the thirty-fourth century before Christ is not impossible." [101]

As for the dating of the Maya culture, Egerton Sykes thinks that its representatives arrived on the American continent (from overwhelmed Atlantis?) with an enormous scientific baggage, and adds: "The usual assumption that they had picked up in a hundred years or less the knowledge which it took the Western World two thousand or more years to acquire seems to me to be unrelated either to historical precedent or to common sense." [102]

This reasoning is valid for many other peoples: the Aztecs, for example, knew very well that the celestial bodies were spherical in form and imitated their movements in their games; the African Dogons spoke of the "dark companion of Sirius," discovered only by the use of telescopes; and the ancient Mediterranean peoples knew some of the Pleiades which are invisible to the naked eye (see Fig. 112).

The Babylonians knew also of the existence of the four great moons of Jupiter; Io, Europa, Ganymede and Cal-

Fig. 267. These Etruscan monuments at Chiusi seem to recapitulate the idea of step-pyramids and of "special sculpture" so widely diffused throughout the world.

listo. "Until the invention of the telescope by Galileo," says J. E. Gore,[103] "mankind was totally ignorant of these satellites."

There are only two possible explanations. One, that the Babylonians must have possessed telescopes, seems too farfetched, even though in the British Museum there is a remarkable piece of crystal, oval in shape and ground to a plano-convex form, found by Sir Henry Layard during his excavations of the Palace of Sargon at Nineveh. Sir David Brewster suggested that the disc was a lens even though most scholars reject his theory.[104]

Referring to Indian and Chinese discoveries, Tomas writes:

"For centuries the Brahmins have zealously guarded the astronomical table of *Surya Siddhanta*. In this textbook on the astronomy of ancient India the earth's diameter was computed to be 7,840 miles. The distance of the earth to the moon was calculated at 253,000 miles. The figure accepted by modern astronomy for the equatorial diameter of our planet is 7,926.7 miles, and the maximum distance to the moon is known to be 252,710 miles. From these figures it can be seen how remarkable was the accuracy of the ancient astronomers of India, especially at a time when Europeans were suffering from a "flat-earth" complex. The date of the *Surya Siddhmata*'s last compilation is about A.D. 1000, yet some Hindus believe that earlier editions were in existence about 3000 B.C. If so, the book is all the more puzzling. . . .

"The *Huai Nan Tzu* book (c. 120 B.C.) as well as the *Lun Heng* of Wang Chung (A.D. 82) outline the centripetal cosmogony in which 'whirlpools' solidify worlds out of primary matter. These writings of ancient China give a preview of modern ideas on the formation of galaxies.

"Thus we are faced with two alternatives; either to admit the existence of superior astronomical instruments in antiquity, or to assume that the priests of Babylon, Egypt and India were the custodians of a prehistoric science at least ten thousand years old."

X

Gilgamesh

There lived at Erech [105] a being, two-thirds divine and
one-third human. He was Gilgamesh, a character scarcely
to be recommended, sometimes cold, sometimes impulsive,
who always managed to get his own way, the more so as
it seemed impossible to better him in fight. His fellow
citizens put up with him for a short time, but in the end,
tired of what they considered abuses of power, they en-
treated the Lord of the Sky to free them from this arrogant
pest.

The Lord of the Sky entrusted the task to the goddess
Aruru, she who had created man from clay, and Aruru,
once more making use of the same material, molded a
creature which she called Enkidu. Some defined him as
"half human, half animal," other described him simply as
a very powerful savage, all muscle and hair. Enkidu confronted Gilgamesh and struck him down. Filled with admiration at the courage of his adversary, he was, however,
forced to recognize the limitations of brute force.

Thus the two became friends. Gilgamesh assumed the
role of "brains" and decided to celebrate the alliance by
eliminating the monster Humbaba who was lying waste
the surrounding countryside.

From the very beginning this episode presents elements
only apparently mythological; the creation of man from
clay (or from "mud"?) is common to too many peoples
separated by great distances of space and time to be merely

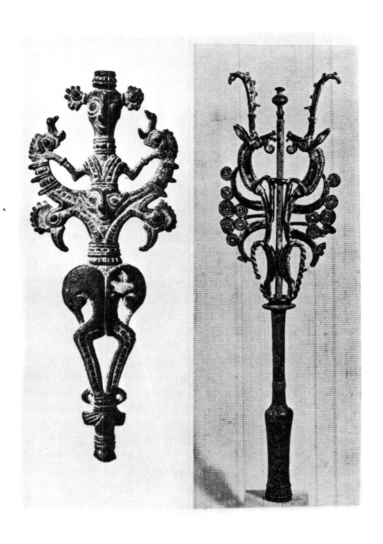

Fig. 268. It was in this way that the mountaineers settled
in the north of Mesopotamia depicted Gilgamesh.

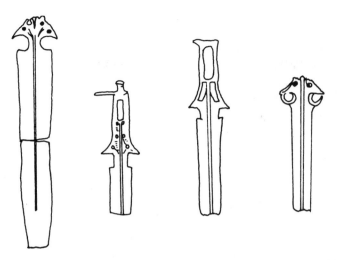

Fig. 269. Sardinian sword-hilts from Monti sa Idda, Decimoputzu.

Fig. 270. Axes in the form of birds from the early Anatolian Bronze Age found near Mahmutlar.

335

a fable, and reflects an aspect of scientific fact; that of the formation of life from inert material. In the story of which we are speaking,[106] we can see two creatures of differing origin: Gilgamesh, born on another planet ("two-thirds divine," that is to say, come from the skies) and adapting himself to life on this globe ("one-third human"), and Enkidu, son of Earth, still very primitive ("half human and half animal"). Gilgamesh, wayward and intelligent, provided with talents and weapons which allowed him to impose his own will, was perhaps taken by surprise by the other and was subdued by brute force. Here is the being from the stars transformed into a civilization-cultivating hero, assuring himself of the friendship and collaboration of Enkidu, that is to say, of the terrestials, and acting in their common interest against other creatures.

Let us take a look at the strange images of Gilgamesh *Fig. 268* handed down by the mountain peoples settled in the north of Mesopotamia; wings, bird's heads, solar symbols, spirals, all juxtaposed in complex and highly significant symbolism.

Very interesting comparisons have been made with findings from all over the globe and common elements have been noted in an enormous number of objects more or less simplified, elaborated, stylized, according to the cultural and artistic level of the countries concerned.

Fig. 269 The sword-hilts found in the Nuraghic repositories of Monti as Idda (Decimoputzu), with very strange designs resembling flying creatures and solar symbols, come from a Sardinia for which we have been unable to provide a *Fig. 270* date. From the Anatolian early Bronze Age we have axes in the form of the bird of Mahmutlar, whereas the head of the Mesopotamian Gilgamesh (see Fig. 268 on the left) appears to have been reproduced in a Frankish buckle comparable in some respects with the two idols from Vidra *Fig. 271* near Bucharest.

Fig. 272 These last, in their turn, bring us back to the bizarre "spacials" of Tell Ashmor, also in Mesopotamia, and, across the ocean, to the Peruvian "diadem of Pachacámac."

336

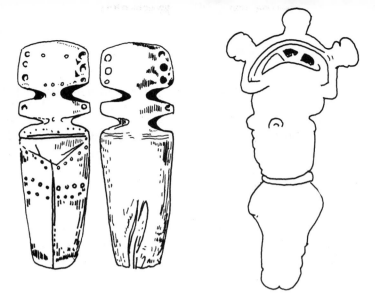

Fig. 271. (Above) On the left two idols from Vidra near Bucharest; on the right a Frankish buckle.

Fig. 272. (Below) Curious Hittite "divinities" with conical triangular heads from Tell Ashmor in Mesopotamia. They are comparable with the strange diadem found at Pachacámac near Lima (on the right).

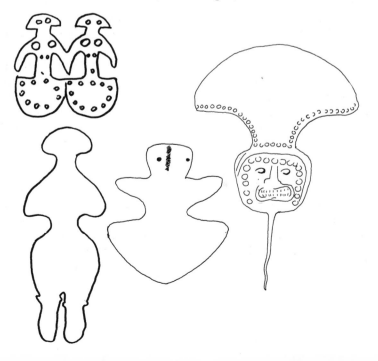

Fig. 273

Fig. 274

From that country comes also the ritual knives with similar handles, similar solar symbols and similar Mediterranean spirals. If we look at the photographs reproduced here, we shall not fail to recognize the strange thread that links them across innumerable miles and innumerable centuries.

Lords of time

Fig. 275

But who was Humbaba? If an illustrator of Utopian tales were asked to create a monster alien to customary forms, he would not be able to do better than the unknown creators of the terracotta of Abu Habbah, which goes back to the seventh or eighth century B.C. They present us with a creature which it would be very difficult to imagine, a mask which makes any attempt at interpretation very questionable.

Is it a question of yet another being brought down from space? We might be inclined to believe the adventure of the two heroes. They found themselves, in fact, faced with a "forest" blocked by a doorway. They succeed in crossing the threshold but, as if by incantation, the door itself closes behind them, crushing one of Enkidu's hands.

From this to the idea of an automatic device is only a short step. And techniques of this sort are by no means unknown; doors which open and close themselves, shutters which close automatically, images of gods which rise up as if by magic, have been described countless times in the ancient Mediterranean world and Theodor Gaster in his book *The most ancient stories of the world* tells us how tales of this kind are diffused in the Harz Mountains, in Asia and in Iceland.

Having vanquished Humbaba with the aid of the Sun god, Gilgamesh has a meeting, which at first sight could seem pleasant, with the beautiful goddess Ishtar, who promises him, in exchange for his favors, a "gold chariot" which will bear him to "the dwelling place of the gods." Our hero, however, must have known the temptress pretty

Fig. 273. An Inca bronze knife found at Cuzo in Peru.

Fig. 274. Another "ritual knife" represents a Chimu mythological personage. Note the resemblance to the Cuzco knife, the solar symbols and the spirals.

well, for he reproaches her that she has never been sincere and has never shown even a minimum of fidelity to her admirers.

"You have loved a lion," he tells her, "and seven times you have dug its grave. You have loved a stallion and yet have subdued it with whip and spurs."

We think that the sexual perversion known as "zoo-philia" has very little to do with these episodes. Perhaps the science fiction version would be more acceptable: Ishtar, she too comes from the cosmos, asks the aid of other "shipwrecked astronauts," only to abandon them after taking advantage of their abilities.

The terrible stellar vamp certainly does not submit passively to this affront; she unleashes against Gilgamesh "a furious bull descended from the skies," which, however, is killed by Enkidu.

We are in full interplanetary conflict. The "gods," friends of Ishtar, do not delay taking their revenge for Gilgamesh's reaction to a liaison which would make possible his return, if not to his own globe, then at least to worlds more advanced than the one in which he has landed. Unable to strike at him directly, they hurl themselves against the far more vulnerable terrestial. Enkidu, according to the legend, has a dream.

"It seemed," writes Gaster, "that a great clamor arose in the heavens and on the Earth and a strange, horrible creature with the face of a lion and the wings and talons of an eagle descended from no one knew where and carried him off. Then suddenly, feathers sprouted on his own arms and he assumed the same appearance as the creature that had assailed him."

Are we faced with a cosmic rape? It is not easy to decipher the passage which has been greatly distorted in different versions. Enkidu goes away and Gilgamesh, after lamenting his friend, thinks of his own skin, making his way to an island "placed at the ultimate confines of the Earth" on which lives "the mortal who has escaped

Fig. 275. The monster Humbaba, vanquished by Gilgamesh, on a terracotta from Abu Habbah (7th-6th century B.C.).

death," the very old Utnapishtim. He is faced by mountains, whose passes are defended by monstrous creatures, and enters an impassable tunnel. The hero then turns to a woman innkeeper and learns that to reach Utnapishtim he must cross an ocean, "the ocean of death" on which man has never sailed.

The protagonist of our epic is not frightened; he reaches his goal and meets the "great old man" who, in a version very similar to that in the Bible, tells him the story of the

341

Flood. And it was a Flood truly universal, contrary to what has been asserted up to a short time ago by Biblical scholars induced to see in the notes attached to the Old Testament a local inundation, relatively small.[107] "Would that famine had wasted the world, rather than the Flood," comments Utnapishtim, the "Sumerian Noah."

In some versions he survives, adapting himself to the new circumstances created by the cataclysm. Here we seem to hear an echo of the *Mahabhârata*, the famous epic of ancient India, the longest in the world: "When the fish was thrown into the ocean by Manu, he spoke these words to it: 'O most blessed one, you have procured me an entire and continual right of self-preservation. Now learn from me how you must act when the time comes. Very soon, O blessed one, all that is stable and noble in terrestrial nature will undergo a great and general transformation, a complete dissolution, O most blessed one.' "

It was a prediction of the Deluge, a statement that man would not be able to escape the disaster except by "changing into a fish," that is to say, confronting a new situation in a new way. Many scholars consider that from just that situation would be born various mythological figures which Fig. 276 we see, perhaps, already expressed by the fishhooks of Easter Island in the form of tritons. The Indian "Makara" Fig. 277 from the *stupa* of Barhut dates from the first century B.C.; it is a marine monster with a tail in the form of a spiral and with the solar symbol beneath its jaw. It appears to ex- Fig. 278 press an idea similar to that of the Etruscan siren, with feathers like wings, facing a "tree of life."

Gilgamesh is searching for just this tree, the existence of which is revealed to him by Utnapishtim. "On earth there is nothing eternal," he said, but added: "In the depths of the sea there exists a plant which looks like a hawthorn. If a man gains possession of it he can, by tasting it, recover his youth."

Was it the famous "tree of life," everywhere symboliz-ing the aspiration to an indefinite longevity and at the same

Fig. 276. Easter Island fishhooks in the form of tritons.

Fig. 277. The Indian "Makara," a marine monster with spirals and solar symbols. Perhaps a representation of the Flood.

Fig. 278. (Below) A very beautiful Etruscan siren. Note the tail in spirals with the "tree of life" in front of it.

343

Fig. 279
time flight, space, the stars? We shall be induced to assert this unhesitatingly when confronted by the motifs that accompany it on a Scythian vase of the sixth century B.C. found at Chertomlyk in the Ukraine—a winged star, birds, spirals, flowers, the heads of lions.

Fig. 280
We see the same trees scratched on the rocks among the innumerable graffiti in the Valley of Marvels (Alpes Maritimes). Some archaeologists claim to be able to discern in them "human faces in linear technique," but it is very probable that they are in fact just the "magic plant," since we see it, reproduced in the same way, in various parts of the world.

Fig. 281
Ishtar herself, with finger pointing at the "tree of life," before which stands a personage with a star above his head, may be seen on an Assyrian cylinder-seal of the first mil-

Fig. 282
lennium B.C.; and in the Hypogeum of Tutmoses III at Thebes, the king is being suckled by a "sacred tree." Of the hieroglyphs which can be discerned on the left, the solar symbol and the scarab, symbol of immortality, stand out.

Fig. 283
Together with other motifs which recur throughout the globe, the enchanted plant also dominates the "hall of the Bucintoro" on Isola Bella (Lake Maggiore), whereas other figures directly recall the oriental dragons and the birds of the ancient American civilizations.

Fig. 284
We find it also in times considerably closer to our own, even though the original significance has been lost. Thus,

Fig. 285
among the objects of value preserved in the Como museum we see in a clear and very beautiful stylization what could be its branches crossing and intertwining to form outlines of spirals and solar symbols.

Fig. 286
Here trees and flowers unite, whereas in a Phoenician incense-burner, in the form of a little temple, the lotus flower unfolds at the top of the plant.

Is this the symbolic flower of Gilgamesh? Let us say clearly: yes. In antiquity the name was given to various floral types, very different from one another: the Egyptian

Fig. 279. (Opposite page) A Scythian silver vase foun at Chertomlyk. As well as the "tree of life," it has a the familiar elements of "mysterious archaeology."

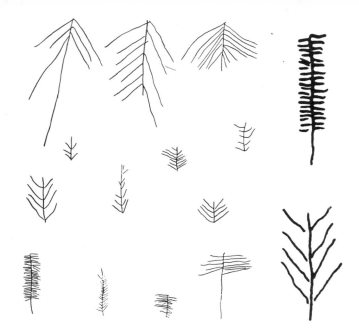

Fig. 280. The "trees of life" of the Valley of Marvels (Alpes Maritimes).

Fig. 281 (Below) Ishtar standing before the "tree of life"; an Assyrian cylinder-seal of the first millennium B.C.

Fig. 282. The Hypogeum of Tutmoses III (Thebes);
the sovereign is suckled by a "sacred tree."

Fig. 283. (Below) Together with other motifs recurrent
throughout the world the famous tree is also to be found
in the "hall of the Bucintoro" at Isola Bella (Lake Maggiore). Other designs directly recall Chinese dragons
and the mythical birds of pre-Columbian America.

"lotus" was in fact a water-lily (*Nymphaea alba*), the Hindu one was a lotus-lily (*Nelumbo nucifera*), to cite only two of the innumerable examples. It is transformed into "wheels of the law" on imprints of the feet of Buddha, into solar and stellar symbols in the exhibts in the Como museum; and in the strange fragments built into the walls of the facade of the town hall of Osimo (Ancona). The Etruscans elaborate it in the most varied forms, and it is preserved in the West, even to our own days, becoming the rose window of Christian churches.

But let us return to Gilgamesh. The hero succeeds in getting possession of the magic plant, but while he is bathing in a mountain stream a serpent snatches it from him.

"Often," writes Gaster, "there have been incorrect interpretations of the final episode in our story. It is the general opinion, in fact, the Utnapishtim tries to make Gilgamesh's disappointment less biter by showing him the way to obtain a plant which grants immortality. But this does not correspond to the original text, and an interpretation of this nature destroys the real significance of the episode.

"The plant in question is not one granting immortality, but only one which closely approaches it, a plant which restores youth to the old and decrepit and which, for just this quality, makes more tolerable the pain of being mortal."

We seem to hear re-echoes of some verses of the Aztec songs:

Does one really live here on Earth?
Not for all time, only for a little!
As you know, so too do I know; we live only once.
One day we shall go hence.

and again:

Oh, if we should live forever!
Oh, if we did not have to die!

"The belief in a plant of this sort," continues Gaster,

Fig. 284. A "tree of life" of comparatively recent date, with interlaced serpentiform designs in the Como museum.

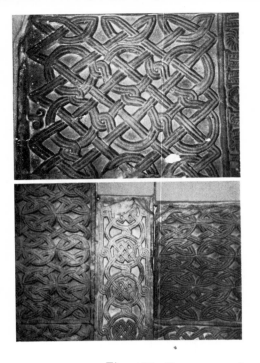

Fig. 285. Other serpenti-
form designs from the
Como museum.

Fig. 286. Once more in the Como museum, "rosettes"
alongside "trees of life."

Fig. 287. A Phoenician incense-burner in the form of a small temple with the "tree of life" surmounted by the "solar lotus."

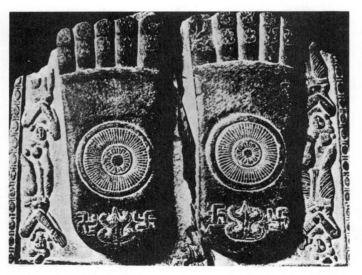

Fig. 288. Footprints of Buddha, with the "wheel of the law."

Fig. 289. "Rosettes," serpentiform plaits, wheels and solar symbols from the Como museum.

Fig. 290. Built into the facade of the Osimo (Ancona) town hall can be seen knots of serpents, solar symbols and signs recurrent in very many places and going back to a remote past.

Fig. 291. "Rosettes," stylized lotus flowers, spirals and crosses on four interesting Etruscan finds.

Fig. 292. The so-called "wheel of fortune" in the cathedral of S. Vigilio at Trento.

"is common to the popular traditions of many parts of the world. The *haoma* of ancient Iranian mythology is sometimes represented as a plant which grows on an island of Lake Vurakasha. The moisture which it secretes possesses the quality of dispelling senility and renewing all things. And as in our story, the plant was eaten by the serpent, so in the Iranian myth Ahriman, the power of evil, created a firefly to feed upon the plant itself. Also the *soma* of Indian belief is a sort of elixir of life contained in the moisture of a plant of paradise."

What if it were not a question of a plant but of a substance indispensable to an astronaut shipwrecked on earth, whose life, though destined to come to an end, had a longer duration than the life of terrestials?

And should we see in the serpent a cosmic vehicle crewed by beings in no way inclined to prolong the existence of Gilgamesh?

And did. Wilson Tucker in his novel *The Time Master*,[108] make use of science fiction terms to retranslate events made legendary in the memory of the ancients?

Atlantis still lives

Utnapishtim is not an invented character, nor for that matter is Noah, whom we meet throughout the world, sometimes under his familiar name; in Hawaii he is Nu-u, in China Nu-Wah and in the Amazon region Noa.[109] In Paraguay and in Brazil he is Tamanduare and in Mexico Tapi or Nalà (with his wife Neua). He becomes Pokawo for the American Delaware Indians, Manibosho for the Canadian Redskins, Zeu-Kha among the Patagonians, Yima in Persia, Dwifah in the Celtic legends.

The concept of evil-doing men punished by a Deluge recurs in innumerable traditions, from those of the Wiyot-Wishosk, of the Pomo and of the Mattole of California (all now extinct) to the Pawnees of Nebraska, who worship Tirawa, the "Spirit Father" to whom they attribute the extermination of a perfidious race which "did not want to recognize him."

Human ingratitude also aroused the anger of the creator of the Yaghan, a people settled in the Tierra del Fuego and now almost extinct. Their legends provide two versions of the catastrophe; one speaks of intolerable cold, incessant falls of snow, vast stretches of ice-floes, the other of violent inundations. It is obvious that the former does not exclude the latter, and the link can be found when it speaks of the Sun which "shone once more after a very long night" but did not succeed in melting all the glaciers, though restoring hope in existence even after other "terrible destructions." [110]

Lissner comments that, very probably, the Yaghan legends refer to catastrophes which really took place about ten thousand years ago and links them to the descriptions of the Deluge given by the Kato Indians of California: "It rained, it rained every day. Every evening, every night, it rained. It rained too much, people said. They now had no fire. The streams filled, the water rose in the valleys, the water surrounded them on every side. All people went to sleep. Then the sky fell down. There was no more land. The waters of the ocean covered the whole earth. All the grizzly bears died, all the elks drowned, all the panthers drowned, all the deer drowned; all animals drowned."

"Except for the Arabs, the Kaffirs and the Blacks (not the Masai), ancient traditions of an immense inundation are to be found everywhere," writes Hennig. "In 1891 Andrée listed eighty-five legends of this type. Since that time many others have been traced, so that today we know more than a hundred. If we reject those which could have been inspired by missionaries, there remain sixty-eight which are native. Thus, Asia provides us with thirteen accounts of the Deluge, Europe with four, Africa with five, Australia and Oceania with nine and the "new world" with thirty-seven: sixteen in North America, seven in Central America and fourteen in South America." [111]

Shall we summarize some of these traditions, other than those already cited? Here they are, reduced to almost telegraphic terms. The Eskimos (like the Chinese) still have to this day a legend which tells how the Earth was "violently shaken" by an "immense deluge in the course of which many people drowned."

We read in a Maya codex that "the sky approached the earth and in one day all perished. Even the mountains disappeared under water." In ancient Mexico, moreover, an event in the distant past in which "the constellations took on a new appearance" was regularly commemorated.

The Guatemala Indians remember "a black rain which fell from the sky at the same time as an earthquake de-

356

stroyed houses and caves"; the Amazon Indians tell how, after a tremendous explosion, "the world was plunged into darkness"; and the Peruvian Indians add to the same story that "the waters reached the tops of the mountains."

The Venezuelan tribe of white Indians, the Paria, whose "capital was a village with the significant name of Atlan, had a tradition of "a great disaster" which destroyed their mother-country, "a vast island in the western sea."

Andrew Tomas quotes a papyrus of the twelfth Egyptian dynasty of three thousand years ago, preserved in the Leningrad Hermitage, which mentions the "Island of the Serpent" and contains this passage: "After you leave my island, you will not find it again as this place will vanish under the sea waves." And, referring to another testimony of the sons of the Nile, he adds: "Once a star fell from heaven and the flames consumed everything. All were burnt but I alone was saved. However, when I saw the mountain of corpses I almost died of grief."

The Hebrew writer and philosopher Philo of Alexandria (30 B.C.-C. 50 A.D.) in his book *De Incorruptibilitate Mundi* writes: "Consider how many regions (not only those close to the coast, but also those inland) have been swallowed by the waters, and consider what vast expanses of land have become seas, plowed only by innumerable ships. Who does not know of the famous isthmus which in ancient times united Sicily with Italy? When the seas from either side, agitated by violent tempests, met one another, the land between them was submerged and carried away . . . and for that reason Sicily, which was at first part of the continent, became an island.

". . . and the island of Atlantis, which was larger than Libya and Asia combined, as Plato says in his *Timaeus*, was submerged in a day and a night by the sea, following furious earthquakes and floods. . ."

Let us come to later times and hear John Swain declare in his *Speculum Mundi* (1644): "I think that America was at one time part of that great country which Plato calls

Atlantis and that the king of that island was in touch with the inhabitants of Europe and Africa. . . ."

In the eighteenth century a theory of this nature was accepted by the French naturalist Buffon, and in the nineteenth by the German traveller and geographer Von Humboldt.

The learned Ignatius Donnelly (1831-1901), lieutenant governor of Minnesota and a member of the United States Congress for eight years, maintains in his books *The Antediluvian World*, *Pagnarok* and *The Age of Fire and Ice* that the Maya civilization originated in that of Atlantis and, in 1882, set out his theory in thirteen points:

1. At one time there was in the Atlantic a large island called Atlantis by the ancients, the residue of a still vaster region.

2. The description by Plato is not a fable but history.

3. Atlantis was the cradle of civilization; it was there that man emerged from barbarism.

4. From overpopulated Atlantis, peoples emigrated to the Gulf of Mexico, reached the Mississippi, the Amazon region, the South American Pacific coast, the Mediterranean, the western coasts of Europe and Africa, the Baltic, the Black Sea and the Caspian.

5. The antediluvian world was Eden, the garden of the Hesperides, the garden of Alcinous, Mesomphalos, Olympus and Asgard; all these fabulous places were merely memories of a world in which men lived in peace and happiness.

6. The gods and goddesses of ancient Greece, of the Phoenicians, of the Hindus, of the Scandinavians, were simply the kings, queens and heroes of Atlantis. Whatever has been attributed to them in mythology is only a confused memory of historical events.

7. Egyptian and Peruvian mythology mirror the original religion of the Atlantides.

8. The most ancient Atlantide colony was probably Egypt, whose culture mirrors that of the mother country.

9. The utensils of the European Bronze Age derive from those of the Atlantides who were the first men to work iron.

10. The Phoenicialn aplhabet, mother of all the European alphabets, was derived from the Atlantide alphabet and was transmitted also to the Mayas.

11. Atlantis was the seat of the Aryan, or Indo-European peoples. It was also the seat of Semitic, and perhaps the Turanian peoples.

Fig. 293

12. Atlantis was destroyed by a terrible catastrophe; the island sank into the ocean together with almost all its inhabitants.

13. A few persons managed to save their lives on ships or rafts, reaching the coasts to the east and west and bringing with them the legend of the Deluge.

As if foreseeing the skeptical attitude of future readers, Plato stresses that his account is "strange, yet perfectly true." The geographical description of what must have been the principal island of the Atlantides is very exact.

It must have been a sort of quadrilateral about 370 kilometers (592 mi.) long and 185 kilometers (296 mi.) wide,[112] surrounded by high mountains.

Fig. 293. This stone with a clearly Semitic inscription was found in the state of Tennessee.

"Whether by the action of nature or by the work of various kings," writes the Greek philosopher, "a canal was excavated which surrounded the entire plain. What is said concerning the depth, the size and the purpose of such a canal is difficult to believe, as is also the fact, that a work carried out by the hand of man could have had such dimensions.

"It is therefore necessary to state the canal was 30.826 meters (99.9 ft.) deep, 148.8 meters (491.04 ft.) wide, and 1,850 kilometers (29.60 mi. long.[113] It received the waters of the streams which came down from the mountains, made a complete circuit of the plain, encircled the city and thence flowed into the sea. From the upper part of this canal rectilinear channels about 30.80 meters (101.6 ft.) broad were rut in the plain and joined the canal itself close to the sea. Each of these channels were 18.5 kilometers (29.6 mi.) from the next, and across channels were cut between them to bring to the city seasonal products or timber from the mountains. . . ."

Fig. 294   This ancient description has made it possible to reconstruct the general plan of what must have been the capital of the Atlantides.

Should we want a "live" idea which, more than anything else, could induce us to accept Donnelly's hypo-
Fig. 295   thesis, we should go to Barbury Castle in Wiltshire. In its neolithic perimeter we shall see reflected the plan of the legendary metropolis!

"Atlantis really existed," declares the Muscovite physicist and mathematician N. Lednev, after twenty years of research. "It was an immense island extending for hundreds of kilometers (640 mi.) to the west of Gibraltar." [114]

"The existence of Atlantis is not impossible or unacceptable from a geological standpoint," affirms Professor V. A. Obrutchev of the Soviet Academy of Sciences. "Soundings in the northern part of the Atlantic Ocean may reveal underwater ruins of buildings and other remains of an ancient civilization." [115]

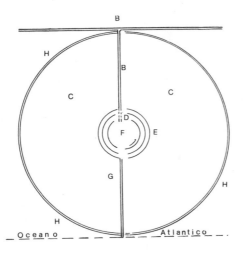

Fig. 294. Plan of the capital of Atlantis, according to the ancient texts. A: irrigated plain; B: irrigation canal; C: city area; D: bridge; E: gate; F: acropolis; G: navigable canal and H: perimeter wall.

Fig. 295. (Below) The neolithic perimeter wall of Barbury Castle in Wiltshire strangely recalls the plan of the Atlantean capital.

361

Ekaterina Hagemeister, also of the Soviet Union, wrote in 1955 that since the waters of the Gulf Stream reached the Arctic Ocean between 10,000 and 12,000 years ago, Atlantis must have been the barrier which diverted the current to the south. Atlantis was the cause of the appearance of the Ice Age. Atlantis was the cause of its end.

Further confirmation of the hypothesis formulated in earlier works [116] comes to us from Professor N. S. Vetchinkin: "The fall of a gigantic meteorite was the cause of the destruction of Atlantis. The impact of gigantic meteorites are clearly visible on the surface of the moon. There are craters 200 kilometers (320 mi.) in diameter . . . Falling into the sea, gigantic meteorites brought about tidal waves which washed away not only the plant and animal kingdoms but also hills and mountains." [117]

It is probably a result of this cataclysm that the rotation of the terrestial globe was thrown into confusion. Let us refer once again to some evidence from Andrew Tomas:

"Martinus Martini, seventeenth-century Jesuit missionary in China, wrote in his *History of China* about her oldest records. These speak of a time when the sky suddenly began to fall northward. The sun, moon and planets changed their courses, after the earth had been shaken. . . .

"The Harris Papyrus mentions that the earth had turned over in a cosmic cataclysm. The Hermitage Papyrus of Leningrad and the Ipuwer Papyrus also allude to the world having turned upside down.

"The Indians living in the lower reaches of the Mackenzie River in northern Canada maintain that during the Deluge an unbearable heat wave came upon their arctic land. Suddenly the heat was followed by a severe frost. A displacement of the atmosphere in an earth tilt could have brought about the weather extremes spoken of by the Canadian Indians."

A displacement which led to an inversion of the apparent motion of the sun. We have already said this, but we can now add some additional evidence: let us restrict

Fig. 296. (Above) Representation of a Celtic musical instrument preserved at Capodimonte (Naples); below, a graffito from High Moor (Yorkshire). They seem to show the two opposing directions of apparent solar movement.

Fig. 297. (Below) Solar wheels, clockwise and counter-clockwise, in juxtaposition (Como museum).

Fig. 296

Fig. 297

ourselves to the "solar wheels" whose movements, clock-wise or counterclockwise, are shown not only in the swastikas reproduced and cited in *Not of This World*, but also in the designs of Celtic musical instruments, which correspond to English graffiti and even to Italian reliefs whose creators certainly did not have even the faintest memory of that remote cataclysm.

No reply

1562: Diego de Landa, bishop of Yucatan, consigned to the flames all the Maya manuscripts which had fallen into his hands. At that time he considered them "devilish texts"; but the passing years brought wisdom to him. He tried to save what could be saved, within the limits of the possible, from the senseless auto-da-fé. He could be seen sitting, night after night, foregoing sleep and defying hunger, beside his former most bitter enemy, the highly cultured King Cocon, both now preoccupied only with extracting from the obscurity of the past passages from the Maya records. With the aid of the ruler, of an old pagan priest and of other wise men, de Landa succeeded in reconstructing the ancient calendar, though imperfectly, since his knowledge of the idiom in which his former adversaries conversed had a number of gaps.[118]

For more than two and a half centuries, however, nothing more was heard of his discoveries.

1850: A learned missionary working in Guatemala, Etienne Brasseur de Bourbourg, who was by chance in Madrid, borrowed from a library a book which interested him. It was a book which, in all probability, had interested few before him since the eccesiastic when consulting it, saw a few unbound sheets slip from its pages. They were the lost manuscript of Diego de Landa!

This discovery would have been very important in itself, but the future, reserved for the lucky scholar another extremely pleasant surprise: On a stall in the market in Mexico City, where books were being sold by weight, he acquired for four pesos a work unique in the world—a copy of the largest Maya-Spanish dictionary ever compiled.

This afforded him the opportunity of editing a guide to the Maya script which drew the attention of very few but which enabled him to translate the so-called "Troan Codex."

The words which, in the course of his labors, the missionary interpreted, despite the errors and incomprehensible terms of the text upon which his translation was based, must have left him dumbfounded. They outlined a catastrophe of enormous scope: ". . . and the lord of the earth raised up, the lord of the pumpkin failed, the land was raised up by the red monster . . . and the lord of the earth swelled the land beyond measure, the lord of the waters . . ."

The allusions to telluric phenomena ("the earth raised up," the "pumpkin failed," this last an image which suggested the idea of deformation), to volcanic eruptions (the "red monster"), to inundations (the "lord of the waters"), to subsidences and rapid elevations of the land, were very evident, so much so that Brasseur immediately thought of an extraordinary analogy with the *Critias* and the *Timaeus* of Plato.

Were the Maya referring to Atlantis?

No. They knew of the cataclysm which caused the submergence of the lands of which the Greek philosopher was speaking, but they had recorded it in another passage: "The calamity took place on the eleventh day of Ahau Katun. . . . there fell a most violent storm of rain and ashes from the skies and in a single great wave the waters of the sea poured upon the Earth. . . . the skies fell and the solid earth sank. . . . and the Great Mother Seyda was among the memories of the destruction of the world." [119]

The catastrophe alluded to in Brasseur's summarized description was another one and the missionary became aware of this when translating the name of the region which disappeared when "the lord of the earth raised up"; according to de Landa's alphabet it was pronounced *Mu*.

Fig. 298

And the Maya letters have their equivalent in the symbol found in Asia by James Churchward which was intended to designate the legendary sunken continent in the Pacific! He was a strange figure, this Churchward, and we say this with no hint of sarcasm. The well-known British colonel had, in fact, the indubitable merit of having collected a quantity of valuable material which was taken into consideration by official science only to a minimal degree, and at that, very unenthusiastically. There are, however, attenuating circumstances as Churchward later turned to the study of esoteric doctrines, which made it very difficult to distinguish between the real and the fantastic elements of his work.

It must, however, be admitted that the tablets studied by Churchward in India and Tibet show astonishing

Fig. 299

analogies with the Australian "Brothers of the lightning" and some Maya finds, with the inscriptions on the calendar-stones of pre-Columbian America, the designs incised on the Tizec monoliths and on the "stone tables" of Azco-potzalco. They are enough to support, in a far from indifferent manner, the hypothesis of the existence of a vast extension of land in the Pacific which was subject to various upheavals, the last of which (perhaps the cataclysm which destroyed Atlantis?) caused its total disappearance from the face of the globe.

When the star of Baal fell on the place where now is only the sea, the seven cities trembled with their golden gates and their temples. A great gust of hot air arose and the streets were filled with dense smoke. Men trembled for fear and a vast crowd thronged the temples and the king's palace. The king said: "Did I not predict all this?" and the men and the women, all clothed in their finest clothes ornamented with precious jewels, prayed and implored him: "Save us, Ra-Mu!" But the king replied that

366

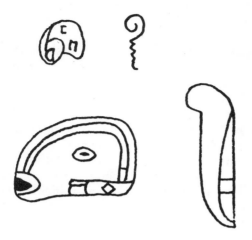

Fig. 298. (Above) The sign of Mu discovered by Church-
ward. (Below) the Maya alphabet according to de Landa
As can be seen, the letters M and U are very similar to
Asiatic symbols.

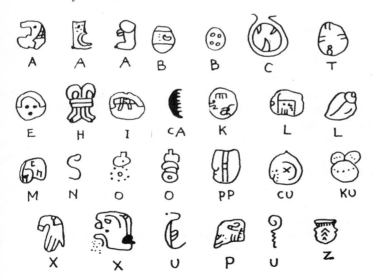

A	A	A	B	B	C	T
E	H	I	CA	K	L	L
M	N	O	O	PP	CU	KU
X	X	U	P	U	Z

they would all have to die, together with their slaves and their children, and that a new race would be born from their ashes.

Thus, according to Churchward, the Lhasa tablets recorded the final catastrophe, cause by the fall of a celestial body, identified by some as an asteroid. Pure fantasy? We would say no, considering the enigmatic archeological finds which strew Asia and the Pacific islands.[120]

The colonel claims to have been able to establish, by his research, that the empire of Mu rose more than a hundred and fifty thousand years ago and attained its greatest splendor about seventy-five thousand years ago when colonizers emigrated from its seven principal cities either in the direction of Atlantis or towards central Asia. Here they laid the foundations for what would later (about 20,000 B.C., still according to Churchward) be the great empire of Uighur.

Perhaps it is only a bizarre coincidence, but we must remember that another Uighur empire arose in the tenth century A.D., claiming very remote traditions. Settled first in Mongolia and then in Chinese Turkestan, its creators, the Uighurs themselves, attributed their origin to a culture which disappeared with the Mongol conquest of the twelfth century.

As to the supposed expansion of Mu towards the American continent, we shall see its ultimate traces in the logs of the navigators who, sailing the Pacific, came across strange islands which have never been seen again. The Spanish Juan Fernandez (discoverer of the island to the west of Chile to which he gave his name, and of the Desventuradas, S. Felice and S. Ambrogio) said, for example, that he had landed in 1576 on the coast of a "continent" situated in the vicinity of Easter Island, traversed by "very broad rivers". and that he had been spellbound by contacts with "people so white and so well dressed."

Inventions, hallucinations, errors?

Fig. 299. The extraordinary Australian graffito of the
"Brothers of the lightning," beings which seem to be
wearing astronauts' helmets, overalls and boots.

No. In such tales there is always something that is true,
even if those who spread them were persuaded for obvious reasons to rose-tint the places and peoples whom
they met in their interminable voyages who were closer in
character to those already known to them.

It could be that fragments of these submerged lands
might have continued to exist until relatively recent times,
only to disappear, they too, beneath the waves.

Returning to great Mu and still following the account
of the British officer, we see it as a land of widespread
forests and meadows with a subtropical climate, with
mastodons, peopled by sixty-four million inhabitants be-

longing to ten different races. The heirs of the most advanced among these will be us, and our ancestors of the lost continent will have left us as a heritage a vaguely bronze coloration, thick black hair and blue eyes.

To what point is this story credible? We cannot say. What has struck us, however, is the news that Dr. F. Brue Russell, a psychoanalyst of Los Angeles, has found near St.˙ George in Utah mummies which he claims have come from Mu.

Gilgamesh, if in truth he still lives, could tell us something more.

Fig. 300   But perhaps he would not have eyes or words for a mankind which would refuse to believe him.

Fig. 300. (Following page) Find from Amorgos in t Cyclades (c.2500-2000 B.C.).

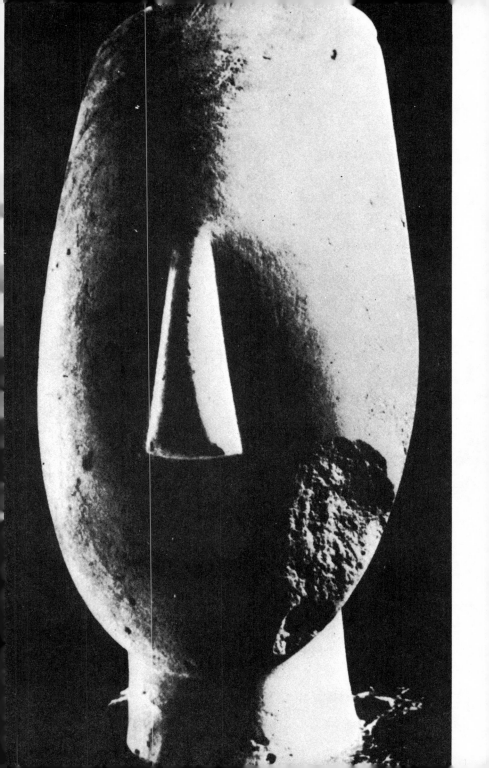

Notes

1. We shall return more fully in a later book to the remarkable activities of this association, which includes among its founders, Dr. Mario Zambelli (who has made many important discoveries) and Professor Dario Fogliato, one of the greatest authorities on the Roman provinces.
2. "Paleolithic UFO shapes," *Flying Saucers Review*, Vol. 16, No. 2, May-June, 1970.
3. Ivar Lissner, *Aber Gott war da*, Walter-Verlag, Olten, 1960. English translation: *Man, God and Magic*, Jonathan Cape, London, 1961.
4. *Non E Terreste*, by Peter Kolosimo, Sugar Editore, Milan. English translation: *Not of This World*, University Books, New Hyde Park, N.Y., 1971.
5. *Terra Senza Tempo*, by Peter Kolosimo, Sugar Editore, Milan. English translation: *Timeless Earth*, University Books, New Hyde Park, N.Y., 1973.
6. Nicola Turchi, *Storia delle religioni*, Sansoni, Florence, 1963.
7. Stone buildings, circular in form, common to many ancient civilizations.
8. *Galaxy*, New York, 1959.
9. Mimmo Castellano, *La valle dei trulli*, Leonardo da Vinci Publishing House, Bari, 1964. (Text by Leonardo Sinisgalli, Giuseppe Cocchiara, Enzo Minchilli).
10. *Not of This World*, op. cit.
11. We shall deal more fully later on with this strange creature and the "special" references connected with it.
12. *Not of This World*, op. cit.

13. *L'alba della civiltá*, Mondadori, Milan, 1961.
14. *Not of This World*, op. cit.
15. *Il pianeta sconosciuto*, by Peter Kolosimo, Sugar Editore, Milan.
16. G. Lingé, *Nouvelle Zélande*, Paris, 1971.
17. *Timeless Earth*, op. cit.
18. Roger May, *Passport pour l'insolite*, La Palatine, Geneva-Paris, 1960.
19. *Smena*, No. 8, 1961.
20. Andrew Tomas, *Atlantis—From Legend to Discovery*, Robert Hale, London, 1972
21. J. Alden Mason, *The Ancient Civilizations of Peru*, Penguin, 1957, as quoted by Andrew Tomas in *Atlantis*, op. cit.
22. *Scientific American*, N.7-298, June. 1951.
23. *Smena*, No. 8. 1961.
24. Denis Saurat, *L'Atlantide et al règne des géants*, Editions J'ai lu, Paris, 1969. English translation: *Atlantis and the Giants*, Faber and Faber, London, 1957.
25. Andrew Tomas, *Atlantis*, op. cit.
26. A. H. Verrill, *Old Civilizations of the New World*, The New Home Library, New York, 1943.
27. J. L. Mitchell, *The Conquest of the Maya*, Dutton, New York, 1935.
28. *Not of This World*, op. cit.
29. *Il pianeta sconosciuto*, op. cit.
30. E. Tongiorgi—N. Lamboglia, *La grotta di Toirano*, Instituto nazionale di studi liguri, Bordighera, 1967.
31. Ivar Lissner, *Man, God and Magic*, op. cit.
32. *Timeless Earth*, op. cit.
33. *Not of This World*, op. cit.
34. Andrew Tomas, *Atlantis*, op. cit.
35. Richard Hennig *Les grandes énigmes de l'univers*, Robert Laffont, Paris, 1957.
36. *Timeless Earth*, op. cit.
37. Roger May, *5000 siècles de mystères*, La Palatine, Paris—Geneva, 1959.
38. Louis Charpentier, *Les géants et le mystère des origines*, Robert Laffont, Paris, 1969.
39. *Das Buch des Rates*, *Popol Vuh*, Eugen Diederichs,

374

Verlag-Düsseldorf-Colonia, 1962, quoted in *Not of This World*.

40. Theodor H. Gaster, *Le storie più antiche del mondo*, Giulio Einaudi, Turin, 1960.

41. Discovered in spring 1970.

42. April 29, 1971

43. *Ombre sulle stelle*, by Peter Kolosimo, Sugar Editore, Milan.

44. Nicola Turchi, *Storia delle religioni*, Vol. I, Sansoni, Florence, 1963.

45. *Timeless Earth*, op. cit.

46. Theodor H. Gaster, *Le più antiche leggende del mondo*, Giulio Einaudi, Turin, 1960.

47. Nicola Turchi, *Storia delle religioni*, op. cit.

48. Denis Saurat, *Atlantis and the Giants*, op. cit. Menhirs are rough monoliths set vertically in the ground, whereas, dolmens are formed by a great slab set across rocks embedded in the soil, and cromlechs are made up of menhirs placed in a circle.

49. As is logical and well known (we have been asked to develop the argument more deeply later), the idea of human flight is almost always expressed by the symbol of a bird.

50. Jullian, *Historie de la Gaulle*, Hachette, Paris.

51. G. Lilliu, *La civiltà dei Sardi dal neolitico all'età dei nuraghi*. ERI, Turin, 1967.

52. Vari, *La civiltà del mistero*, Mondadori, Milan, 1963.

53. Roger May, *5000 siècles de mystères*, op. cit.

54. Pierre Honoré *Ich fand den weissen Gott*, Verlag Heinrich Scheffler, Frankfurt-am-Main, 1961. English translation: *In Quest of the White God*, Hutchinson, London, 1963.

55. At first a colony of Sybaris, then Lucanian and then Roman, in the eastern part of the Gulf of Salerno, strangely called by the Greeks "Poseidonia."

56. The photographs from which two of these subjects were taken have been reproduced in *Timeless Earth*.

68—431—Spaceships in Pre-History

57. Andrew Tomas, *Atlantis*, op. cit.

58. *Timeless Earth*, op. cit.

59. *Not of This World*, op. cit.

60. R. N. C. Bowen, *The Exploration of Time*, George

Newnes, London, 1958. Quoted from Andrew Tomas, *Atlantis*.

61. *Timeless Earth*, op. cit.

62. *Timeless Earth*, op. cit.

63. He was the son of Aegeus and Aethra. It seems to us of interest to refer to the writings of Felice Ramorino in his *Classical Mythology* (Hoepli, Milan, 1967): ". . . but since Aethra was loved by Poseidon, Theseus was also called the son of Poseidon. If it is considered that Aegeus was identified with Poseidon, it is easy to understand that Theseus, Son of the Sea and of Aethra, otherwise the dawn calm, was a personification of the Sun."

64. As we shall see later, the reference to rain is also symptomatic.

65. It was doubtless located in the extreme north. "They inhabited a region in which all was dark and wrapped in an eternal twilight . . . but the Sun illuminated it" is admitted by Simonides, Hesiod and Pindar.

66. Magistrates with duties similar to those of the Roman consuls.

67. Louis Charpentier, *Les géants et le mystère des origines*, op. cit.

68. Ivar Lissner, *Man, God and Magic*, op. cit.

69. Oswald O. Tobisch, *Kult, Symbol, Schrift*, Verlag für angewandte Wissenschaften Baden-Baden, 1963.

70. All the poetry quotations are taken from the *Canti Aztechi (Aztec Songs)* edtied by Ugo Liberatore and Jorge Hernandez-Campos (Guanda, Parma, 1966). Some of the songs, read by Alberto Lupo, are on the record of similar title in the "Collana letteraria Documento" (CL 0514). The numbers in brackets refer to the songs listed at the end of the quotations themselves.

71. *Only for a little.*

2. *Like the spring grass.*

3. *At least the flowers.*

4. *Song of sadness.*

5. *Song for the ancestors* (Tlapalla is "the place of Red and Black" and "marks the path of the Sun from its zenith to its setting").

6. *Lonely as a cloud.*

376

7. *The doubt.*
8. *Song of Xipe Totec, the drinker of night.*
9. *The kingdom of death.*
10. *To the god of war, Huitzilopochtli* (the names *Amantia* and *Pipitlan* indicate the sea and the southern section of the sky respectively).
11. *The poet's torment.*
12. *The song of Tetlepanquetzanitin.*
13. *Song of friendship.*

72. *Timeless Earth* and *Not of This world*, op. cit.
73. B. Laufer, *Prehistory of Aviation*, Field Museum of Natural History, Chicago, 1928.
74. *China Pictorial*, Peking, No. 8, 1958.
75. *China Reconstructs*, Peking, August 1961.
76. Nicholas Roerich, *Vrata v Budushschie (Gateway to the Future)*, Uguns, Riga, 1936
77. The interior of New Guinea. A good example is that of seven thousand planes brought down over its forests during World War II. Only about a hundred could be located (v. *Il pianeta sconosciuto*). Quoted from the weekly *Der Erzähler* (Austria).
78. P. H. Fawcett, *Exploration Fawcett*, London, 1953.
79. Mari was an ancient city on the Euphrates, whose ruins were found near Abu Kemal near the Syrian-Iraqi frontier. According to the list of Sumerian kings it was "the tenth city to exercise royal rights after the Deluge."
80. A *lebes* is a vessel used to heat, or to keep hot, water mainly for libations.
81. Theodor H. Gaster, *Le più antiche storie del mondo*, op. cit.
82. Nicola Turchi, *Storia delle religioni*, op. cit.
83. *Not of This World*, op. cit.
84. *Vie Nuove*, June 29, 1962.
85. *Not of This World*, op. cit.
86. Louis Charpentier, *Les géants et le mystère des origines*, op. cit.
87. Andrew Tomas, *Atlantis*, op. cit.
88. Andrew Tomas, *Atlantis*, op. cit.
89. *Corriere del giorno*, February 15, 1970.
90. *Timeless Earth*, op. cit.

91. C. N. Mehta, *The Flight of Hanuman to Lanka,* Narayan Niketan, Bombay, 1940. Quoted from Andrew Tomas, *Atlantis,* op. cit.

92. Andrew Tomas, *Atlantis,* op. cit.

93. I. Idriess, *Drums of Mer,* Angus and Robertson, Sydney, 1962.

94. *Smena,* Moscow, coll. 1960-70.

95. *L'Unità,* May 7th, 1971.

96. Ivar Lissner, *Man, God and Magic,* op. cit.

97. *Timeless Earth,* op. cit.

98. *Timeless Earth,* op. cit.

99. Funerary vases.

100. *Timeless Earth,* op. cit.

101. Richard Hennig, *Les grandes énigmes de l'univers,* op. cit.

102. *Atlantis,* July-August 1966, London.

103. J. E. Gore, *Astronomical Essays,* Chatto & Windus, London, 1907.

104. W. B. Carpenter, *The Microscope and its Revelations,* J. & A. Churchill, London, 1891.

105. The biblical names of the Sumerian city of Uruk, 225 kilometers (350 mi.) southeast of Bagdad, where there are ruins of a colossal step-tower.

106. Various versions of the Gilgamesh epic exist. The most complete was discovered in the library of Assurbanipal; it dates back to the middle of the third millennium B.C. but, after comparison with more ancient versions, it appears to have been greatly revised.

107. *Timeless Earth, Not of This World, Il pianeta sconosciuto,* op. cit.

108. Published in Italy by Mondadori in the collection *Urania* under the title *Signori del tempo (Lords of Time),* May 30, 1954.

109. For a complete list see *Timeless Earth,* op. cit.

110. *Il Mare,* Instituto Geografico de Agostini, Novara, 1971.

111. Richard Hennig, *Les grandes énigmes de l'univers,* op. cit.

112. Here, as later, the Greek measures are rendered in metric terms.

113. The figure is obviously inexact; it must have been an error of transcription.

114. *San Francisco Examiner*, July 14, 1958.

115. E. Andreyeva, *V poiskakh poteriannogo mira (In search of a vanished world)*, Detgiz, Leningrad, 1961.

116. *Timeless Earth, Not of This World, Il pianeta sconosciuto*, op. cit.

117. *Teknika molodezhi*, Moscow, Nos. 9-12, 1956.

118. See *Mu* in the encyclopaedia *Il Mare* of the Instituto Geografico De Agostini, Novara, 1971.

119. The translation is by the Brazilian philologist O. M. Bolio (1930).

120. *Timeless Earth*, op. cit.

Relationship
seminar
Vide tapes

1(800)862√500